BOOKS AND
THE TEEN-AGE READER

BOOKS
AND
THE TEEN-AGE READER

A Guide for Teachers, Librarians, and Parents

G. ROBERT CARLSEN

HARPER & ROW, PUBLISHERS
NEW YORK, EVANSTON, AND LONDON

FIRST EDITION

LIBRARY OF CONGRESS CATALOG CARD NUMBER: 67-13685

Contents

Chapter 1
The Reading Experience

In the highest civilization, the book is still the highest
delight. He who has once known its satisfactions is provided with a resource against calamity.

Emerson

A man can live but one life, and each of us lives his
life in a tiny capsule of time and space from which he
cannot escape. A man's life span is short indeed compared with the thousands of years of human civilization. A man's living space is a tiny pin point on the
globe. He is limited by the cultural ideas automatically
imposed upon him by his environment.

But through the miracle of books, man can break
these bonds. On the library building at the University
of Colorado is engraved the motto: "Who knows only
his own generation remains forever a child." And to
know more than our own generation, we must turn to
books. Only then can we find what life was like and
how men thought in the Golden Age in Greece, at the
high point of the Roman Empire, during the sudden
flowering of culture in the Renaissance, in the periods
of violent revolution that produced the concept of
democracy.

Even the most avid traveler can visit only a small
portion of the world and come to know only a few
peoples. But through books we can break geographical
as well as historical barriers. The more we read the
more we understand people who live a thousand miles

away or one hundred miles away; and we begin to realize that each people considers its own locality the center of the universe no matter how undesirable a place it appears to the outsider.

Man is a story-making and story-enjoying animal. One seldom meets an individual who does not like stories about real or imaginary people. Furthermore, man is curious: he enjoys discovering facts and inventing theories, explanations, and relationships.

All of us tend to do those things we do well and to avoid doing those things we do poorly. This same tendency is shown in adolescents' reading habits. The poor reader does as little reading as possible and gets the least satisfaction from what he does read, while the child who reads well is inclined to seek out books and spend much of his spare time reading. Consequently, the good reader experiences the rewards of reading, and tends to improve his skills; the poor reader falls further behind his age and grade level.

Learning to read is one of the most complex tasks that a human being accomplishes in his lifetime. The amazing thing is not that a few people fail, but that so many succeed. We recognize that one child may learn to swim better than another, that another can excel in playing a musical instrument, but we expect that all youngsters can be made to read equally well. The assumption is false. Just as the child with excellent body co-ordination has a better chance to excel in sports, so a child with a high level of intelligence has a higher reading potential.

As a parent you are perhaps only dimly aware of how well your adolescent son or daughter reads. You may take it for granted that your child learned to read well in elementary school. Yet a child may go on for several years and even reach secondary school without having his reading deficiencies detected. Usually records on a child's reading ability are kept, but they are not always used.

By the time he reaches secondary school, the student may be one of one hundred and fifty to two hundred students with whom the teacher meets each day. The classroom provides little time or opportunity for individual reading problems. Also, a child may do a fairly good job of covering up deficiencies: he gets a friend to tell him what the assignment was about; he even finds out how to bluff his way through book reports and library assignments.

How do you find out if your teen-ager is equipped with good reading skills? And if he is not, what can you do about it?

Most schools give a reading test which can provide parents with a reading score expressed by a grade equivalent. Such an interpretation indicates whether the child is reading at his grade level, above it, or below it. If the score is expressed as a percentile, 50 per cent of the students will fall between the twenty-fifth and seventy-fifth percentile level, and you can judge the score of your child accordingly.

Some eighth-grade students will be reading four years ahead of their grade level, some four years below. By the time students are in the eleventh grade there will be a ten-year differential between the best and the poorest readers.

Nevertheless, those things young people want to read about are related to their chronological age regardless of the level of their reading ability. Therefore, an eighth-grader who has twelfth-grade reading ability, does not usually have twelfth-grade reading interests, nor does the one with a fourth-grade reading ability have fourth-grade reading interests, a problem that will be dealt with in Chapter 3.

In addition to the standardized tests, there is another, perhaps less accurate, but still useful, way to find out about your child's reading ability: ask him to read aloud from one of his textbooks. Oral reading demonstrates whether your child can read along fairly smoothly, whether he recognizes the basic structural patterns of the English sentence. Oral reading also indicates a child's comprehension; it may even show something of how he attacks an unfamiliar word. If a child has trouble with the flow of the sentences and stumbles over the pronunciation of words, his understanding of the book's contents may be poor. One other simple test is to ask your child to read a thousand words of a textbook silently and then to summarize the material. Since most adolescents should be able to read nontechnical materials designed for them at least at 300 words per minute, you can estimate a student's speed and comprehension by this device.

What can you do to help your son or daughter improve his reading skills? First, find out what facilities his school provides. Schools often have reading clinics to which a student may be assigned for a few hours each week. Sometimes there are also specialized classes for students with reading problems. Or you may want to look into the professional help in the community. Private tutoring *can* boost a student's reading ability.

Let's assume that your tenth-grade teen-ager has the reading skills of a fifth-grader. You are alarmed about this deficiency, but remember that a fifth-grader can read a great deal. He can read the daily newspapers, almost any popular magazine published in America, most of the popular novels selected by the various book clubs, and a variety of manuals giving directions —the great bulk of printed material that forms the reading fare of the average adult. On the other hand, he will probably be having considerable trouble with the literature in his English classes and with assignments that require reading in the standard research sources; he may even have difficulty reading social studies texts. Hence, if his future reading needs are those of the average adult, his reading level is not as alarming as it sounds; but if he is considering further education, he has a serious reading problem.

This young person will probably be helped most by being given books to read that are exciting and interesting to him and that he can master easily. Here the parent plays a crucial role.

Books and the Teen-age Reader demonstrates how one goes about giving good reading experiences to young people, leading them one step at a time up the ladder of reading enjoyment. Each rung upward leads towards more mature and demanding reading materials. The chances are good that your child's reading skill will grow in direct proportion to the degree of success and enjoyment he finds in books. Hence, it is truly important to help an adolescent learn the excitement and satisfaction of reading. Fortunately, much is known about the process that produces a reader, particularly among adolescents. Studies seem to indicate that adolescence is the crucial period in developing the habit of reading. Certain kinds of reading experiences seem to build enthusiasm for books; other kinds of experiences generally seem to kill enthusiasm.

The following general principles, to be elaborated later, apply to creating pleasure in reading:

1. Enjoyment of what one reads is essential if the individual is to continue to read at an adult level.
2. Boys often want to read one kind of book; girls, another kind. This division, according to sex, often continues into adult life, but it is then less dramatically obvious than it was during adolescence.
3. Young people go through reading phases. These remain relatively the same from child to child, but certain children pass through particular phases more swiftly than others.
4. These reading phases are probably related to the basic psychological problems the adolescent is facing at different stages in his growing up.
5. Enthusiasm for reading can be stimulated. A child can be helped but not forced toward reading maturity.

6. Reading material must be available.

With these basic principles in mind, the parent can make the home atmosphere more conducive to an enthusiasm for books.

1. The child should see his parents reading. Although the adolescent may be highly critical of the adult world, his image of it is shaped by what his parents do. If the parent never reads, or scorns reading, the young person will not care about reading. On the other hand, the adolescent who knows that his mother occasionally gets so absorbed in a book that she forgets to iron his shirt, or who is aware that his father reads regularly before going to sleep, is likely to feel that reading is important in the adult world.

2. The adolescent should hear books discussed. Although reading is an intensely personal activity, it has social implications. People who enjoy reading generally seek out others who like books and discuss the books they've read. Make books the subject of casual discussions at the table during dinner, in the car while on an errand, or at the sink when doing dishes. State your reactions to the author's treatment of the subject. Argue that the problem presented was unreal or frivolous. Express the feeling that a book is blatant sensationalism. But share your ideas, your feelings, about the books you are reading. Avid adult readers report that they grew up in families where books and ideas were part of everyday family life.

3. Books and magazines should be readily available. Most young people surrounded by reading materials will read. A reading home will have books piled on the coffee table, magazines stacked in the bathroom, and novels lying on the floor beside a bed. Obviously the adolescent should be encouraged to seek out books for himself, but at first the parent may need to encourage his interest by bringing books from the library, or buying inexpensive paperbacks. Paperbacks are marvelous sources of good reading material; their small size and attractive covers may tempt a young person to try them.

4. *Reading should not be forced.* The adolescent, in rebellion against the adult world, will tend to reject things pressed upon him by an adult, especially if told they will be "good for him." Some parents require reading a book as the price to be paid for going to a football game or a movie, or for watching television. This approach succeeds in associating books with the unpleasant and usually drives the young person away from the very activity the parent intends to encourage.

In our culture there is the feeling that to finish a book once it is started is some kind of virtue or obligation, but nothing could be further from the truth. It is a sign of maturity to recognize that a book does not appeal to you and to put it aside. Such an attitude should be encouraged in the adolescent, for often he begins a book that is too complicated or sophisticated for his stage of development. A good reader is one who reads perhaps twenty pages and then decides whether the particular book deserves more of his time or not.

Adolescents are sometimes made to feel guilty because they do not enjoy the body of literature called "classics." Adults sometimes seem to feel that books are like cod-liver oil or spinach, the more one gags, the better the results. Such a parent insists his teenager struggle through *The Return of the Native* though the youngster dislikes every page and simply does not understand what it is all about. The parent assumes that such forced reading will improve his adolescent's reading tastes, but this assumption has no basis in fact.

5. *The community should provide adequate school and public libraries and bookstores.* A guide to the adequacy of each type of library has been set up by the American Library Association. How well your child's school library measures up to these standards is, in general, a matter of arithmetic. For example, the ALA recommends that a school library in small schools

have a collection of 6,000 to 10,000 books. This does not mean that the fewer the students, the fewer the books necessary; a school of 200 students may need and make use of 10,000 books more intensely than a school with 1,000 students. A rule-of-thumb figure calls for a library to have 10 books per student enrolled.

Another figure to consider is the budget allocated for the purchase of books. The library budget should be somewhere between $4 and $6 per student for the purchase of books each year.

The ALA also recommends that a library be readily accessible, be located in a quiet spot away from the distracting noises of gymnasium or playground, and be used solely as a library, not as a study hall.

Another factor important to the adequacy of a library is the caliber of the individual in charge. His training and ability are important to efficient administration, to systematic acquiring of books, and to developing students' reading interests. A trained librarian should be provided for every three hundred students enrolled.

Whether your school library meets these standards will depend to a considerable degree on the demands of the parents in the school district. Enlightened parents can do much to change a school library rating from poor to very good. It is easy for the casual parent to be blinded by the "prettiness" of the library. Though the space is often cheerful and attractive, this virtue may obscure the sad truth that the actual number of books on the shelves and the size of the room and staff are inadequate for the size of the student population which must use them.

A prime source of reading matter for your youngster is the public library. In a good public library young adults should be encouraged to use all materials. There are some libraries with special places and/or special collections for the adolescent reader. An understanding librarian with special training in this area will be able to guide the young reader.

Outside the metropolitan area bookstores are few. Almost all readers feel pride in owning their favorite titles, and adolescents usually have strong desires to own those books that mean a great deal to them. Book clubs sometimes serve this need. Scholastic Book Services offers paperbound books geared to children's and adolescents' needs and interests. It operates entirely through book clubs in the schools. Two of the clubs—Campus and Teen Age—serve adolescents. Periodically, a series of titles is announced, and the student may order as many as interest him, but he is not obligated to buy any set number of books for the year.

The bookstores operated within the schools either by a service organization or the students themselves have proved immensely popular with the student population. Such stores may be opened for only brief periods in the morning, at noon, and after school. Books, usually paperbacks, are stocked because of their high level of appeal to the adolescent reader or because they fit the school's curriculum. Parents, working through the PTA, may well be instrumental in starting such a store if the school does not have one.

Commercial bookstores and secondhand bookstores are fascinating places to the initiated, but the adolescent may bypass them because he feels insecure when visiting them. A good bookstore permits its customers to browse without a clerk's constantly urging them towards a purchase. To help your teen-age son or daughter overcome his feelings of strangeness in a bookstore, take him with you the next time you visit one. There he can see how people pick up books from tables and shelves and read the blurbs on the book jackets, how they skim here and there, tasting first this book and then another, how they ask clerks for certain kinds of information. Through such firsthand observations the young person discovers how to browse in a bookstore and how to select titles that promise satisfying reading.

Too much parental encouragement may kill the enthusiasm parents are trying to generate, and too little show of interest may have the same discouraging result. Reading is a treasure that cannot be forced on the young person, yet he needs help to find his way to its inherent rewards. You cannot *make* your child enjoy reading. You can only hope by example, by interesting discussions of books, by making materials available, to help him gradually discover for himself that reading "maketh the full man" and the full life.

Chapter 2
The Teen-ager and His World

The imagination of a boy is healthy, and the mature
imagination of a man is healthy, but there is a space of
life between, in which the soul is in a ferment, the
character undecided, the way of life uncertain . . .
                    Keats, *Endymion:* Preface

.

How do books fit into a teen-ager's world? How do
they serve young people's needs? The teen-ager's world
is a highly stimulating world—of folk rock, the Su-
premes, pep rallies, TV, clothing fads, exams, and the
draft. Because of his buying power, the teen-ager has
been wooed by clothing manufacturers, cosmetic salesmen, automobile dealers, and a barrage of peddlers of
self-improvement. To this high-pressured environment
the adolescent brings the complex problems of any
maturing young person.

If books are to have any meaning, they must be related to the young person's personal and social needs.
Keep in mind the steps an individual takes as he grows
from a dependent child to an independent adult.

Some of the basic steps he will take are described
here:

*1. Discovering and accepting his sex's role in our
culture.* Boys must discover what is expected of males,
girls of females. To be sure, in modern society the
stress on equality seems to have dimmed differences
in sex roles, but nevertheless the cultural roles remain
different.

2. Developing new relationships with members of

his own sex. Throughout childhood, friendships are formed principally by the accident of propinquity, but during adolescence old friendships tend to break up and the teen-ager begins to seek his friends on the basis of mutual interest.

3. *Achieving an easy relationship with members of the opposite sex.* Our culture has built a stereotyped picture of the relationship between adolescents. It assumes that the great majority are dating regularly or going steady, and are caught up in a dizzy whirl of social activity. This is not an accurate picture. Many of today's young people do not know how to behave in a social order where sexual mores seem to be changing. Only a relatively small percentage of teen-agers make the easy and relaxed adjustments to the opposite sex that satisfy their own expectations and those of their parents. A girl may build a notion of herself as unpopular and unattractive because she is not dating as actively as the mass media tell her she should be. Many boys find it difficult if not impossible to call a girl and talk casually because they fear rejection.

4. *Accepting his physical body.* As his body grows and changes, the adolescent looks for signs that the ugly duckling is turning into a swan. He believes that his acne will disappear, his teeth straighten, his body gain new and graceful proportions. Whether this transformation takes place or not, during adolescence is the time an individual achieves a workable balance with himself.

5. *Changing his relationship with his parents.* In a short period of six or eight years the teen-ager must succeed in becoming independent of his parents. And parents must accept a different relationship with their child. It is never easy to change a basic human relationship, particularly one established over twelve or fourteen years. The child has been a dependent member of a household in which parents have held the power of decision. This relationship between the child

and each of his parents must now give way to a new relationship of two independent adults, each with an equal right of decision-making. Simultaneously, the adolescent must learn that responsibilities go with the privileges and rights of adult life. Though the parent wants his child to take responsibilities, he is not eager to let his child have the independence of decision that goes with them. During this period, a certain amount of rebellion by the child against the adult world is normal and expresses itself in a number of ways. The young person wears clothing completely different from the current adult styles; he embraces ideas that are antagonistic to established beliefs; he is secretive, and sometimes openly defiant of a parent's authority. These actions are not easy for the parent to accept or to understand, even though he himself once went through such a period of adjustment.

6. *Working for pay.* Part of achieving independence during adolescence is working for money. Each of us can remember that thrill the first time someone outside the family circle paid us for a job. Suddenly we knew we were not completely dependent on our parents for our physical welfare.

7. *Finding a vocation.* The dictionary of occupations lists over two hundred thousand job descriptions. The modern industrial world offers so many specialized occupations that during adolescence the teen-ager should try to discover what kind of jobs he likes to do rather than limit himself to a single vocational experience. Does he want to work with ideas or with people? Or with both? Is he happier outdoors or indoors, in sedentary or active work? Does he prefer routine to variety? Out of such experience and reflection should come a more mature and lasting choice of career.

8. *Becoming aware of his value patterns.* Human beings have infinite possibilities for development. As anthropologists have demonstrated, men value mutual co-operation or competitiveness; cultivate softness or

Spartan harshness, self-centeredness or social responsibility; feel it is important to show one's emotions, or
think it is important to conceal them. Man may strive
for perfection or accept human limitations. The mature
individual must have some sort of integrated system of
values to judge his own actions and those of others.

At the beginning of adolescence, most individuals
do not act consistently. On Monday the teen-ager may
believe in the Boy Scout oath and on Tuesday believe
in the antithetical code of his gang. By the end of
adolescence, however, each individual must come to
terms with his beliefs.

The way each individual comes to terms with himself and society is affected by the specific circumstances of the time during which he matures. From
generation to generation the adolescent rebels against
and flees from the adult world. He feels he is unique;
he is certain no other adolescent or group of adolescents has ever faced the same problems with the same
intensity. The adolescent today believes intensely in his
own individuality and in his right of self-determina-
tion. Today's adolescent doesn't want to wait until he
is twenty-one to begin exercising adult rights. He feels
a sense of isolation and alienation because human relationships in our society are increasingly impersonal.
More and more, both parents work outside the home.
Watching television does not lead to a warm inter-
change of ideas among family members, although it
could and should. Urban life is more impersonal than
was rural and small-town life of the past. The child is
always a member of large groups whether in the classroom or in outside activities. Because of our rapidly
expanding population, the individual is becoming
more and more a statistic. It is no wonder that isolation and loneliness are a dominant philosophical theme
of our time.

In the affluent contemporary society the adolescent
has many more alternatives open to him than ever be-

fore. Therefore, it is possible for him to refuse to follow the path adults propose. Whether he is correct in his thinking or not, he may decide that a spectacular job is waiting for him if he drops out of school. He is confident that if he quits one job a better one is waiting around the corner. He knows that he can probably hitchhike across the country and support himself along the way.

Books may play an important role in helping adolescents reach maturity. They serve in several different ways, seemingly in opposition to one another. Books may become a part of the adolescent's rebellion against the adult world. Often the teen-ager dislikes the reading adults like and praise, and he may scorn their selections. His own favorite authors, the writers for his generation, are usually experimenters both with literary forms and with basic human concepts. Yet literature has always held a mirror up for the reader to see himself sharply and clearly. Literature, by its very nature, is selective and suggests integrations, connections, insights into experience, and values which the individual might not otherwise find for himself. At its best, literature confronts the reader with the basic, eternal problems of human beings, thus helping the individual to see himself as a part of an ongoing history.

Some books present a frontal attack on specific problems the adolescent is facing. These are nonfiction books dealing with problems of sex, dating, grooming, and vocational choices. They are frank and objective in their presentation and are eagerly sought by great numbers of young readers. A selection of self-help books is listed in the bibliography for this chapter.

Bibliography

PERSONAL ADVICE

Archer, Elsie: *Let's Face It.* Lippincott, 1959. A guide to good grooming for teen-age Negro girls.

Bailard, Virginia, and Ruth Strang: *Ways to Improve Your Personality.* McGraw, 1965. Day-by-day building plans for likable, livable personalities.

Bauer, William W.: *Moving into Manhood.* Doubleday, 1963. *Way to Womanhood.* Doubleday, 1965. A doctor proves that getting to be a man or a woman is more, much more, than growing up sexually.

Beery, Mary: *Manners Made Easy.* McGraw, 1966. "No one is born with good manners. They cannot be bought. They must be earned."

Boll, Eleanor S.: *The Man That You Marry.* Macrae, 1963. The girl's role on the "best team that was ever put on earth."

Bossard, James H. S., and Eleanor S. Boll: *The Girl That You Marry.* Macrae, 1960. She's different from a man. She puts home, security, and children *first*. Most of all, she is an individual.

Cain, Arthur H.: *Young People and Drinking.* Day, 1963. To drink or not to drink? Sane facts on alcohol leave the choice to each young person.

————: *Young People and Smoking.* Day, 1964. A poet once called his cigarette "a magic wand"; the Surgeon General called it "a health hazard." Who is right?

Cass, James, and Max Birnbaum: *Comparative Guide to American Colleges.* Harper, 1966. This detailed profile of every accredited four-year college in the nation shows costs and campus life, admission rules, and academic environment.

Clark, Mary E., and Margery C. Quigley: *Etiquette, Jr.* Doubleday, 1965. Proper public and private behavior means never licking fingers, never accepting an invitation from a stranger, and many other never's.

Daly, Sheila J.: *Questions Teen-Agers Ask.* Dodd, 1963.

————: *Teen-Agers Ask More Questions.* Dodd, 1964. A col-

umnist for teens collects the questions asked most often—
on dating, parents, personality, money, and sex.

Doniger, Simon, ed.: *Becoming the Complete Adult*. Association, 1962. Each adolescent is many people—physical,
emotional, spiritual, sexual—and he must get to know
them all.

Duvall, Evelyn M.: *The Art of Dating*. Association, 1958. This
eye-opening approach to dating tackles topics such as
reputation, drive-ins, falling in and out of love, amorous
advances, and interfaith friendships.

————: *Love and the Facts of Life*. Association, 1963. Straight
answers to straight questions on what is normal, what is
healthy, and what is right in matters of love.

Duvall, Sylvanus M.: *Before You Marry*. Association, 1959.
What are the chances for success in marriage? Why do
marriages fail? What about sex in marriage?

Felsen, Henry Gregor: *To My Son, the Teen-age Driver*. Dodd,
1964; Bantam. Sensible advice for the new driver, who
should practice defensive driving.

————: *A Teen-ager's First Car*. Dodd, 1966; Bantam. What
to know about buying a new car and owning it.

Fine, Benjamin: *How To Be Accepted By The College of Your
Choice*. Appleton, rev. 1965; Popular. Excellent discussion
of how to go about preparing for college, making applica-
tion, taking tests.

Goodhart, Robert S.: *The Teen-Ager's Guide to Diet and
Health*. Prentice, 1964. The facts on exercise and nutri-
tion.

Gottlieb, Bernhardt: *What a Boy Should Know about Sex*.
Bobbs-Merrill, 1960. A doctor gives a detailed account of
male sexual development. Dispels many myths.

Gresham, William L.: *The Book of Strength*. Day, 1961. A bar-
bell-dumbbell outfit plus mental discipline can make all the
difference between spindly boys and strong men.

Haupt, Enid A.: *The Seventeen Book of Etiquette and Entertaining*. McKay, 1963. "No one likes to feel awkward or
unsure or ill at ease," says the Editor-in-Chief of *Seventeen* as she presents this insurance against social blunders.

————: *The Seventeen Guide to Your Widening World*. Macmillan, 1965. A girl's widening world of new friends, new
school, and new job demands growth in grace and responsibility.

Jacobs, Helen Hull: *Better Physical Fitness for Girls*. Dodd,
1964. A tennis champion recommends a trim-slim program

which includes push-ups and pull-ups, jumping rope and
the trampoline.

Johnson, Eric W.: *Love & Sex in Plain Language*. Lippincott,
1965. Diagrams and definitions on male-female physiology
and union, fertilization and embryo development, even
birth control methods.

Kaufman, William I.: *1001 Top Jobs for High School Graduates*. Bantam, 1965. An up-to-date guide that proves it
pays to finish high school.

Keiffer, Elisabeth: *McCall's Guide to Teen-age Beauty and
Glamor*. Prentice, 1959. If she's too fat or too thin, too
shy or too sensitive, a girl doesn't need a miracle but only
an honest, do-something-about-it look at herself.

Krosney, Herbert, and Mary S. Krosney: *Careers and Oppor-
tunities in International Service*. Dutton, 1965. People-to-
people contacts on a global scale—in business, social
development, government, religion.

Kursh, Harry: *Apprenticeships in America*. Norton, 1965. With
manpower shortages proving the need for *skilled* workers,
apprenticeship becomes a key route to building, printing,
mechanics-repair, and machining.

Lass, Abraham H., and Eugene S. Wilson: *The College Student's Handbook*. David White, 1965. Ways to avoid becoming a college dropout.

Lorand, Rhoda L.: *Love, Sex, and the Teenager*. Macmillan,
1965. Candid coverage of such question marks as drinking,
masturbation, homosexuality, date behavior.

Lubowe, Irwin I., and Barbara Huss: *A Teen-Age Guide to
Healthy Skin and Hair*. Dutton, 1965. Advice on problems
skin-deep and deeper including acne, allergies, warts, per-
spiration, and sunburn.

McBain, W. N., and R. C. Johnson: *The Science of Ourselves*.
Harper, 1962. Experiments, mental and sensory, explain
the mysteries of human behavior.

MacCloskey, Monro: *You and the Draft*. Richards Rosen, 1965.
Data for draft-age men on enlistment, draft call, and each
of the seven services.

Nixon, Robert E.: *The Art of Growing*. Random, 1962. A profound guide to psychological maturity for the "growers,"
those young people who grow in their "cognitive capacity."

Noshpitz, Joseph D.: *Understanding Ourselves*. Coward, 1964.
A psychiatrist takes teens on a tour of mind and mental
mechanisms, emotions and behavior.

Perkins, Wilma Lord, ed.: *The Fannie Farmer Junior Cook*

Book. Little, Brown, 1957; Bantam. Easy-to-follow recipes for the beginning hostess.

Prudden, Bonnie: *Teenage Fitness.* Harper, 1965. A program of calisthenics and sports designed to transform teens from unfit to fit.

Rankin, William H.: *Be Fit as a Marine.* McGraw, 1963; Cornerstone Lib. A famous Marine colonel shows how to achieve fitness with exercises based on isometrics and isotonics.

Roesch, Roberta: *Money, Jobs and Futures.* Macrae, 1965. With more than twenty-two million teen-agers as competitors, a young person needs to approach summer jobs and lifetime career with planning and purpose.

Roth, Arthur: *The Teen-Age Years.* Doubleday, 1960. Specializing in adolescence, Dr. Roth understands the ailments, diseases, and accidents common among teen patients.

Scott, Judith U.: *The Book of Dating.* Macrae, 1965. Guidelines to all the social situations which bring boy and girl together.

Shedd, Charlie W.: *Letters to Karen.* Abingdon, 1965. Letters to a bride-to-be on how to keep love in her marriage—forever.

Smith, Sally L.: *Nobody Said It's Easy.* Macmillan, 1965. It isn't easy but it's wise for teen-agers to probe their innermost feelings of guilt, fear, frustration, anger, and love.

Splaver, Sarah: *Your Career If You're Not Going to College.* Messner, 1963. To select the *right* job from thousands in the workaday world, the high school grad must do more than flip a coin.

————: *Your College Education—How to Pay for It.* Messner, 1964. Earn while learning, learn now—pay later, apply for scholarship aid, or compete for contest cash.

————: *Your Personality and You.* Messner, 1965. What is personality? Are people born with it? Can it be changed?

Sulkin, Sidney: *Complete Planning for College.* McGraw, 1962. A timetable for college should begin in junior high and end with the placement of a young person in the college suiting his aptitudes, his aspirations.

U.S. Bureau of Labor Statistics: *Occupational Outlook Handbook,* 1966–67. Govt. Printing Office, 1966. This panorama of occupations in the United States today includes job descriptions, qualifications and training, earning and working conditions, and employment outlook.

Wilkens, Emily: *A New You.* Putnam, 1965. Precise pointers

on beauty inside and outside from manners to mascara.
Willis, Ellen: *Questions Freshmen Ask.* Dutton, 1962. Why go
   to college? What are the rules of dorm living? Can I
   maintain my own standards of conduct?
Wilson, Eugene S., and C. A. Bucher: *College Ahead.* Harcourt, 1961; Harvest. Information about government loans,
   tuition, admission, techniques, testing, and placement procedures.
Young, Mary F.: *In Search of Charm.* World Pub., 1965. The
   way people walk or wear clothes, speak or laugh—all contribute to that elusive quality called charm.

HOBBIES

Adler, Larry: *Jokes and How to Tell Them.* Doubleday, 1964.
   A book of good modern jokes with advice on their telling.
Blair, Clay, Jr.: *Diving for Pleasure and Treasure.* World Pub.,
   1960. A group of young men discover and bring up arti-
   facts from a 200-year-old Spanish ship off Yucatan.
Boyd, Mildred: *History in Harness.* Criterion, 1965. An excel-
   lent book for the young person interested in horses and
   racing.
Collins, Henry Hill, Jr., and Ned R. Boyajian: *Familiar Garden
   Birds of America.* Harper, 1965. A copiously illustrated
   book for the bird watcher.
Dixon, Peter: *The Complete Book of Surfing.* Coward, 1965;
   Ballantine. Excellent discussion of surfing in all its varie-
   ties.
Felsen, Henry Gregor: *Here Is Your Hobby: Car Customizing.*
   Putnam, 1965. How to take a stock car and modify it.
Fichter, George S., and Phil Francis: *A Guide to Fresh and
   Salt-water Fishing.* Golden Press, 1965. A guide to both
   fresh and salt-water fishing with copious illustrations.
Fine, Reuben: *The Teenage Chess Book.* McKay, 1964. A com-
   plete book on playing chess for the person just beginning
   to learn the game.
Foss, William O: *Here Is Your Hobby: Skiing.* Putnam, 1964.
   Excellent handbook on skiing.
Glenn, Harold T.: *Automechanics.* Bennett, 1962. Practical in-
   struction for modern auto repair and maintenance.
Hoyt, Edwin, P.: *One Penny Black: The Story of Stamp Collecting.* Duell, 1965. The history of stamps and stamp
   collecting.

Johnson, James R.: *Anyone Can Live Off the Land.* McKay, 1961. How to survive in the wilderness.

LeBell, Gene, and L. C. Coughran: *The Handbook of Judo.* Nelson, 1962; Cornerstone. Manual of instruction in Judo with information about Judo as a sport.

MacFall, Russell P.: *Gem Hunter's Guide.* Crowell, 1963. Complete information about semiprecious stones, where to find them and how to identify them.

MacPherson, Tom: *Dragging and Driving.* Putnam, 1960. Excellent discussion of how to be a knowledgeable and skillful driver.

Patrick, Douglas, and Mary Patrick: *The International Guide to Stamps and Stamp Collecting.* Dodd, 1962. Comprehensive information about stamps is given in question and answer form. A good index makes it easy to find specific information quickly.

Self, Margaret Cabell: *The Complete Book of Horses and Ponies.* McGraw, 1963. A handbook on horses, their care, showing, jumping, and judging.

Ward, Rodger, and Brock W. Yates: *Rodger Ward's Guide to Good Driving.* Harper, 1963; Perennial. In this excellent guide, the authors anticipate difficult driving situations and provide valuable tips for the new driver.

Zarchy, Harry: *Here's Your Hobby.* Knopf, 1950. Easy-to-follow instructions on photography, fishing, ceramics, archery, sailing, painting, and collecting specimens of all kinds.

Chapter 3
The Stages of Reading Development

A man ought to read just as inclination leads him; for
what he reads as a task will do him little good.
                                        Samuel Johnson

Everyone knows that children go through stages as
they grow up. We generally recognize these phases of
growing up, and we know that, difficult as some
of them may be at the moment, they will be outgrown
eventually. Each is a necessary part of the individual's
becoming a whole and integrated person.

Yet, few adults seem to realize that attitudes and ap-
preciations also develop systematically. There is no
such thing as "instant appreciation" of literature, although many parents and educators act as if there
were. Actually, young people move up a series of reading steps that may at last lead them to mature and
sophisticated tastes in literature. Just as the parent accepts the physiological patterns of growth, so he must
accept the reading phases his child will go through to
become a discriminating and enthusiastic adult reader.

Recognition of these adolescent phases of reading is
of the utmost importance, for this is the crucial period
when many potential readers stop reading. Paradox-
ically this is also the period when the young person
may devote more time to reading than at any other
period of his life, provided his interest is not killed.
Furthermore, he usually has considerable blocks of
free time, especially in the long summer vacations, for
intensive reading.

The characteristics of adolescent reading patterns

have been carefully mapped through a number of research studies conducted with thousands and thousands of adolescents, living in all parts of the country and coming from diverse home backgrounds.

According to these studies, chronological age is more important than is mental age in determining what a child will enjoy reading. The average and the above-average thirteen-year-old will be interested in reading the same kind of books. Thus the whole attempt to accelerate the intelligent child by giving him the adult classics of literature does not conform with the facts. Even Jean-Paul Sartre, the great modern French writer, reports in his autobiography, *The Words,* that he read the classics because his family was extravagant in its praise of his precociousness. When he heard footsteps, he says: "I faked. I would spring to my feet, take down the heavy Corneille. I would hear behind me a dazzled voice whisper: 'But it's because he *likes* Corneille.' I didn't like him." He goes on to say that what really appealed to him were trashy adventure stories that his mother bought him by the hundreds. "I owe to those my first encounters with Beauty. When I opened them I forgot about everything."

Preferences are determined not only by age but by sex. There is a real difference between what the teen-age boy and the teen-age girl want to read. By eighth grade, the reading interests of boys and girls are sharply differentiated. And these differences will continue into adult life, for even at a mature reading level men and women tend to select and appreciate different books. It is true that girls and women will frequently enjoy masculine stories, but boys and men will rarely enjoy feminine ones. These sex differences are reflected not only in the kind of story each prefers, but in the type of characters, the plot, the setting, and the time unit within those kinds. Boys want the leading characters to be masculine; girls will read about either sex.

Boys like a large cast of characters; girls, a small cast. Boys like a story with a setting that takes characters half way around the world. Girls like a confined setting on a country estate or in a small town, or in a particular neighborhood. Boys like the intrigue of much action, often involving several different plots; girls like a much more direct and straightforward plot line. Boys' stories usually cover a considerable amount of time while girls' stories take place in a neat time unit: a weekend, a vacation period, or a school year. Boys tend to prefer descriptions of external actions of the characters while girls are interested in the details of emotional reactions. Certainly there are many exceptions to these general tendencies.

Nevertheless, the failure to realize the importance of the reader's sex in determining his reading preferences is evident in the standard English curricula. Because English in the past has been taught largely by women, the selections have tended to be of feminine interest. Perhaps this, as much as anything else, is the reason the schools' literature programs fail to be an exciting, absorbing experience for boys as well as for girls. *Silas Marner, The Lady of the Lake, The Scarlet Letter, Evangeline, A Midsummer Night's Dream,* are all primarily feminine in their appeal. Your son can be driven to dislike reading if you insist that he read *Jane Eyre, Pride and Prejudice,* or *Vanity Fair.*

A third discovery about the reading habits of adolescents is that they generally choose or reject books on the actual subject-matter content of the book. They *will* read books of great language difficulty if the subject lies close to their interests, and they reject even simple books about subjects that bore them. The content that young people between the ages of ten or eleven and eighteen seek in books usually undergoes three transformations.

I. EARLY ADOLESCENCE

This is the period when the child is between the ages of eleven and fourteen, and is in grades five through eight or nine. During this period he will usually find his greatest satisfactions in one or more of the following types of stories.

1. Animal Stories: Often a child who is a passionate reader of animal stories will read as many as 150 to 200 such tales before outgrowing the phase. The really avid reader sometimes becomes specialized. He will read only horse stories or only dog stories or only stories about African beasts. Boys tend to prefer the animal story about the wild and primitive beast in nature such as *The Call of the Wild,* while girls like the animal dependent upon human beings as in *Lassie Come Home.*

2. Adventure Stories: Boys of this age are the biggest readers of adventure tales. Generally the story revolves about a group of young men who find themselves cast adrift in a small boat, or lost on a mountain, or wandering through the wastes of the arctic. The characters must solve their problems through their intelligence and fortitude, attaining a successful solution by the last chapter.

3. Mystery Stories: The adolescent mystery story is quite different from the adult who-done-it. The young reader likes to read about someone almost his age involved in a case of mistaken identity, a robbery, a hunt for a lost will or treasure, or a situation where the "bad" guys are trying to cheat the "good" guys. Boys like their stories to take place in wild and unusual spots such as mountain hideaways, deep canyons, dark forests, whereas girls prefer their stories to be set in a more familiar location such as a deserted house.

4. Tales of the Supernatural: Closely related to mystery stories are these tales that send a pleasant chill up the spine of the reader. Young people thoroughly love being frightened by mysterious accounts of ghosts, zombies, misshapen characters. The weirder the setting, the more eerie the sounds, the better they like it. Graveyards filled with flickering, mysterious lights are a favorite setting.

5. Sports Stories: The story involving baseball, football, basketball, track, and swimming usually hits the high point on the interest scale for boys at this age. Perhaps their own inability to excel in sports during the early teens makes them seek the book in which excellence in physical activities forms the heart of the story. A number of girls at this stage may read some of these stories, encouraged perhaps by their own peculiar family situation or by the interests of the group to which they belong. But although our culture urges girls to be physically active, there are only a handful of stories that center on the girl athlete and her problems.

6. Growing up around the World: Stories of contemporary adolescent life in various countries of the world interest girls especially. They like to compare their own experiences with those of young people of the same age growing up in other cultures. Because these books will probably color the picture of a particular culture that the young reader will carry with him for the rest of his life, they should be accurately and competently written.

7. Home and Family-life Stories: Ever since Louisa May Alcott wrote *Little Women,* the story of a warm and loving family group has been a prime favorite with girls and the type of book most heartily despised by boys. Girls love the romanticized picture of family relationships in which a teen-age girl by hard work, ingenuity, or self-sacrifice pulls her family through a crisis.

8. *Broad, Bold Slapstick:* Both boys and girls glory in the slapstick story. Humor is intimately related to chronological age. What is funny to one age level is seldom funny to another. As adults, we have long ago left behind the adolescent stage of humor. Now it seems utterly stupid. But each new generation has to experience the same stock, humorous situations for itself. Unfortunately, there is not a great deal of material in book form that adolescents find truly amusing. Therefore they turn to television or such a periodical as *Mad Magazine* for this kind of reading satisfaction.

9. *Settings in the Past:* At this early stage of adolescence, girls frequently become devoted to books that have a thin veil of history. These books are not true historical novels. One girl labeled them as "books about the olden times." History is used as a way of leading the young reader into a world different from his own where costumes, customs, and human emotions may be on a higher and more romantic plane than usually experienced in daily life.

As teen-agers near the end of this early stage in reading, boys frequently begin reading two other kinds of books. One of these is the car or hot-rod story in which a boy is intensely involved with a machine and comes to some real understandings about himself. Ordinarily these books also have a strand of competitiveness running through them which is highly appealing to a young person of this age. This is also the period of peak interest in science fiction. Such stories are generally set in the future and deal with explorations of space, exciting developments in the United States, or with people on other planets. Such stories necessarily demand that the reader be willing to pretend and to enter wholeheartedly into an imagined world. Science fiction stories require the very mind set that undergirds all great scientific discoveries in the adult world —the ability to open up the mind to any possibilities. Some of the great books in this area have an imaginative power that previously illuminated only the great poetic romances. Few girls, however, develop any taste for the science fiction story.

II. MIDDLE ADOLESCENCE

By the time the child reaches the age of fifteen or sixteen and is in the ninth or tenth grade at school, the reading interests of the earlier period will have deepened and in some instances changed direction. The selections of boys and girls are probably most different at this stage.

1. The Nonfiction Account of Adventure: Boys, earlier interested in the imagined adventure, will have matured into a more realistic kind of reading interest. In general, they now want a firsthand account from the person who explored a cave, climbed a mountain, sailed alone on a raft, or explored the arctic.

2. War Stories: Springing out of the desire for adventure and closely allied to the adventure stories are the books that deal with men and war. Some of these are fictionalized accounts. Others are actual, vivid recounts of war experiences. Basically boys at this age seem to need to project themselves into situations of great physical and emotional stress, perhaps with the desire to test vicariously their own ability to "take it."

3. Historical Novels: Girls' interest in books about the olden times usually matures at this time into an interest in the longer historical novel. Perhaps *Gone with the Wind* has found its greatest popularity and readership among girls in their middle adolescence.

4. The Mystical Romance: Girls usually hit the peak of interest in the romantic novel at this period. They like a love story in which love takes place between strangely intense people under rather unusual circumstances. *Rebecca* or *Wuthering Heights* are examples of the type of book particularly popular in this category.

5. *The Story of Adolescent Life:* In middle adolescence the reader, both male and female, is most interested in the story that deals with characters a year or so older, living in the kind of community he lives in, and facing the sort of problems he himself is facing. Literature becomes a way of his seeing himself and of testing possible solutions to his own immediate problems. It is interesting that the more the writer gets inside the chief character's mind and feelings, showing his inner struggles, the more popular and enduring the book tends to be.

III. LATE ADOLESCENCE

Late adolescence is designated as that period between the ages of sixteen and eighteen. The young person is finishing his last two years of high school and entering either college or the adult working world. This is the time that as a reader he will have moved into the type of book generally read by adults. However, he is still selective at this particular reading stage, accepting certain adult books and rejecting others.

1. *The Search for Personal Values:* Adolescents are now in a period where they want to crystallize their own value systems. This means searching, questioning, probing, sometimes even destroying. They want to find a personal direction for their lives. Hence it comes as no surprise that the book which centers on an individual struggling to find his values is immensely popular.

2. *Books of Social Significance:* Someone once said that a sure-fire way to insure the popularity of a book for young adults was to center the story on deprived or persecuted persons. There is some validity to the statement, for the young reader is interested not only in finding a set of personal values, but also in finding a code of social values for his society. He responds, therefore, to the book that has as the core of its plot a

picture of economic deprivation, racial inequalities, religious discrimination. These books are often strong, shocking, and sometimes disgusting in their presentation of situations in human life. But generations of young readers have needed to test their social attitudes by reading Upton Sinclair's, *The Jungle,* Victor Hugo's *Les Misérables,* Richard Wright's *Native Son,* and even Harriet Beecher Stowe's *Uncle Tom's Cabin.*

3. *The Strange and Unusual Human Experience:* Moving still deeper and further along the path of personal experience that was first satisfied by adventure and war stories is the book detailing an odd, almost unique experience, often one taking place on the fringes of human life. They may be stories such as *The Snake Pit* that give insights into psychological deviations, or they may center on a person such as the missionary, Tom Dooley, who chooses a way of life strangely different from that of most of us. As the young reader matures, he seems to have an almost insatiable hunger to find out exactly what a human being is capable of, especially under unusual circumstances.

4. *The Transition into Adult Life:* While there is interest in the three areas mentioned above, the book that has the greatest appeal at this stage of the young person's life involves the movement of an individual from adolescence into early adult life. At a moment of change in his own life, the young reader feels the uncertainties of the transition period. How does he move from being a school child dependent upon his parents to being an independent adult caring for himself? He seeks answers by reading books about people facing the same situation. *Arrowsmith* uniquely combines all the appeals discussed here. Centering on a young man in the last years of medical school and the early years of medical practice it is a story of personal values and of social criticism.

Generation after generation of adolescents who ultimately become readers as adults have sought those

books whose subject matter content falls into these
four categories.

But it is also possible to describe the stages of reading in quite a different way. The satisfaction one seeks
from reading changes as one moves toward maturity.
First there is that stage when a reader discovers the
joy of losing himself completely in his reading; he
wants the book to last forever. Reading becomes an escape from daily life so absorbing that he forgets he is
reading at all. He is actually so involved with the characters in the book that he comes back to reality with
a sense of shock. Until a reader has had this kind of
experience with books he will not move on to the
deeper satisfactions of literature. Ordinarily this type
of unconscious delight in reading will occur in late
childhood. Quite frequently it happens with the cheap,
series type of book which will be discussed in the next
chapter.

As the reader matures a bit, he discovers a second
kind of satisfaction in books. Reading becomes a means
of understanding and testing his own problems and his
own world. He reads with a deeply personal sense of
involvement. He wants to read about a person his own
age, somewhat like himself, who is living the kind of
life he himself is living. Books are used as sounding
boards against which the reader tests his own reactions
and seeks for solutions to his own problems. He looks
for a character "just like me" . . . a person "who has
the same feelings that I have." The recognition of self
in books is a continuing kind of satisfaction, even in
adult reading, but the necessity of its being present
fades as one matures.

Next, literature becomes for the reader the avenue
to examining the ongoing philosophical problems of
mankind. In earlier periods of human history and education, the subject of philosophy was one of the major
subjects studied in the schools. In such courses the
individual had a chance to examine the nature of jus-

tice, the problem of death, the search for goodness and satisfaction in living, the issue of human discontent, and the like. In our schools, literature has come to serve this function. Through literature, particularly in the late adolescent period, the reader reads to see how mankind has felt about the great inner problems of being alive. Through discussion of the themes of literature he has a chance to probe the philosophical issues that make man what he is . . . something more complex than a mechanistic functioning organism.

Finally, if one reads long enough he may arrive at a final kind of joy in reading, that of aesthetic enjoyment. The words are exactly right for the ideas they contain; details fit like the pieces of a puzzle into the whole design, and there is a sense that the outcome was inevitable, even though the reader was not able to foresee it.

These stages of satisfaction are usually achieved during the adolescent period. The first stage, that of unconscious delight and complete involvement, happens for most readers in their reading of very unliterary material, the juvenile series books, sentimental romances, or adventure stories. By the eighth or ninth grade young readers are moving out of this phase and beginning to read the adolescent novel which deals with people like themselves. These books are written for the teen-age reader and not for an adult audience. Some of the best adolescent novels reach a significant level as literature. The third stage, using literature as a reflection of the basic problems of humanity, is most often reached when the reader is a junior or senior in high school, and it will probably continue for years. Serious twentieth-century literature is full of this material. Such writers as Hemingway, Camus, McCullers, Steinbeck, and Wolfe open vistas for the reader that he may not have suspected existed. Finally the last stage, aesthetic enjoyment, comes to full flower in the reading of the classics. The mature individual reads the classics with understanding and appreciation, rather than from a sense of duty because he has been told that they are great.

As parents living at the end of the twentieth century, we seem to have a desperate need to force early maturity on our children. We want them to walk early. We hope they will say their first word before the books indicate that they should. We try to teach them to read at two and three. We encourage early dating and adult clothing styles although the children are physically still in childhood. Why are we so eager to have our youngsters grow up? Each of us as an adult should think back to his own childhood. Do we regret having had the opportunity to develop at a slow pace? And while thinking back, it is good to remember our favorite books at given stages of our lives. Are we ashamed that we read *Tarzan* or Nancy Drew? Do we remember how at fifteen we were spellbound by Alexandre Dumas? Were these reading steps necessary to our further maturation as readers? Yes, they probably were. At least the evidence is rather clear that the great majority of people who have become enthusiastic readers went through such steps in the process of growing up. The patterns are amazingly similar for all of us. So our problem in guiding teen-age readers is one of knowing the stages, being ready with the right suggestions when one stage is ending and another about to begin, and recognizing that each stage is but a rung on the ladder toward the truly cultivated human being.

Chapter 4
Subliterature

There's no book so bad but has some good in it.
                                        Cervantes

Works of literature range from good to bad, from significant to insignificant. We often talk of a *ladder* of
literature or of *steps* on a literary scale. At the lower
end of such a scale are kinds of writing that are not
quality literature at all: the frankly sensational book or
magazine, the comic book, the juvenile series book,
and the adult sentimentalized romance and adventure
story. These books may be referred to as subliterature
because the way they are created is quite different
from the way real literature comes into being.

Often the same writer writes both serious literature
and subliterature; Oliver Goldsmith, Theodore Dreiser, and Pearl Buck all wrote "potboilers." Subliterature uses a kind of formula: stock characters, situations,
settings, attitudes, and ideas are manipulated with
slight variations from book to book. The writer can
create this sort of product by filling in details of an
outline without grappling with his own experience or
his own perceptions about life. Usually, subliterature
has a false tone that becomes apparent to the sophisticated reader. All subliterature is not alike. Some of
these books are actually quite skillfully written. A perceptive librarian may refer to a book as being a quarter
of a step or a half a step better than another.

Almost inevitably the child will avidly read comic
books, juvenile series books, and adult potboilers
sometime at the end of the elementary school years

or during the junior high school period. No matter
how good the literary guidance he has had earlier, he
will suddenly find subliterature fascinating. A basic
need in the child at this stage is satisfied by something
in this kind of reading. Therefore it is important to examine it carefully to see why it appeals and how we
can help a child grow beyond it.

THE COMIC BOOK

As every parent knows, few children wait for adolescence to discover the comic books. Actually the peak
of interest comes late in the elementary school. The
comic book grew out of the daily comic strips in newspapers. One of the first of these, "The Katzenjammer
Kids," appeared in a New York paper in the 1890's and
was soon syndicated. Other newspaper publishers
found the idea so appealing to their readers that they
quickly hired cartoonists to draw comics for their own
papers. Because these early strips were all essentially
humorous, the word *comic* became associated with all
work that used the technique of a sequence of pictures
in which a stock group of characters talking among
themselves convey the story line.

The first comic books were collections of actual
strips that had appeared earlier in the newspapers and
were often given away as premiums for various products. The first venture into the commercial comic book,
a paper-covered book produced to be sold at newsstands, came in the early 1930's. These early comic
books were only moderately successful, but by the
mid-thirties they had become a standard part of American culture. The first crime comics made their appearance in the late thirties and when the Second World
War got under way, the popularity of the comic book
zoomed. Perhaps this sudden success was due to the
fact that comics provided cheap, easily accessible, and
portable escape for men under severe tensions. The material was simple, usually full of action, and centered

on dashing heroes and beautiful heroines. Success not only made comics a major American publishing enterprise but also brought about a uniform size and shape for all such materials.

By the 1950's, comics ran the gamut of subjects, characters, language. Many of them were vulgar stories appealing to the worst in human beings by stressing horror, crime, perversion. Some communities became horrified at the kind of thing available for teen-agers on newsstands and brought pressure to bear on retailers to sell only selected comics. As a result, the more vicious and distasteful comics of twenty years ago have all but vanished.

It is, of course, a mistake to assume that all comics are alike. They are no more alike than are their hardbound cousins. Roughly they can be classified into the following types:

Slapstick Comics: These are the descendants of the first comic strips and present ludicrous characters in ludicrous situations. Some of them poke fun at human foibles and society's pretenses, thus serving a real satiric purpose.

Family Life Comics: These are relatively few in number and picture a family group living through daily adventures. Certain standard situations are repeated over and over again: the mother outwits the father, the children outwit the parents, the family has a series of crises with pets or accidents or money troubles.

Hero Comics: Here a central character like James Bond or the Avenger undergoes a series of trials and adventures in which the hero always comes out on top. Sometimes this hero is endowed with supernatural powers, but he is always a magnificent physical type, possessing great intelligence and a keen sense of justice and honesty.

Crime Comics: These are less prevalent than they were in the past. Emphasis is on the criminal, even though he may be brought to his just deserts in the end. In the hero comic, emphasis is placed on the detective and his activities. But in the crime comic the criminal holds the center stage.

Horror Comics: You can usually recognize this type by the picture on the cover of a grotesque monster, a gargoyle-like creature often looming over a frightened girl or being attacked by some audacious young man. These stories are descendants of Edgar Allan Poe's and provide for the young reader that delicious fright that almost all of us have enjoyed at some period in our reading. Analyzed by an adult, the happenings may seem revolting and horrible. But for the young reader such feelings seldom arise, for he never associates these stories with reality. When he picks up such a comic he frankly enters into an imaginary world and the more goosepimples the better he likes the story.

Love Comics: These generally appeal to girls because of the highly romantic, semi-erotic contents. Usually the cover promises more thrills and excitement than the actual story delivers. Girls remain virtuous in spite of dastardly, evil companions and compromising situations. Any similarity to reality is seldom sought or intended. That the heroine must be successful in her romantic adventures is a foregone conclusion.

Educational Comics: Because comic books have proved so popular with the young reader, they have been used for educational purposes. Among the educational comics are simplified versions of the classics, favorite biblical stories, accounts of industrial processes, even reconstructed historical events. Obviously, the amount of information presented through this medium is extremely limited and the coverage shallow. Yet in their way, they may do a good job.

THE JUVENILE SERIES BOOK

Almost as popular as the comics at this stage in reading are the juvenile series books. They have been a part of young people's reading materials in the

United States for a long time. Fifty years ago the Elsie
Dinsmore books, the Horatio Alger stories and the
Little Colonel series were great favorites. The next
generation read *Tarzan*, the Rover Boys series, the
Tom Swift books, and *Honeybunch*. Young people today still read some of these titles, as well as a later
breed—Nancy Drew, Cherry Ames, and the Hardy
Boys Series. These books are written to a set formula.
There is a central character, or perhaps a small group
of characters, who are itching for a good adventure.
No sooner have they voiced this wish than something
unforeseen happens. They find themselves swept up
into a struggle with the "bad guys," who of course
assume different disguises in different books but are
always clearly recognizable as the evil ones. Favorite
settings are a warehouse at night, the confined spaces
of an old corridor in a haunted house, an echoing,
dank cave. Naturally, the hero wins out against overwhelming odds through his ingenuity and courage and
is given very tangible rewards for his cleverness by a
grateful community. Sometimes the series may have as
many as thirty or more books in it. The advantage of
this kind of book for the young reader is that once he
recognizes the pattern he has the comfort of knowing
exactly how the story will turn out. His hero will inevitably win out despite the circumstances, and to the
reader at this period of his development there is a
pleasant security in such knowledge.

ADULT ROMANCE AND ADVENTURE

The third kind of subliterature is the sentimental romance or the adventure story. Such books are generally
written for adult consumption. They are often serial-
ized in women's magazines prior to publication or appear as originals in the paperbacks on the newsstands.
The older titles were written by such writers as Zane
Grey, Grace Livingston Hill, Harold Bell Wright, and
Gene Stratton Porter. Modern versions of this type

have the same elements as the earlier ones. There is usually a great deal of action; the characters are "superlatives" of their particular type . . . the most beautiful, the handsomest, the most courageous, the most brilliant. The ending is a happy one and exactly what the reader might hope would evolve. It is not surprising that today a number of these books deal more frankly in eroticism than did their forerunners.

The adult may wonder why this subliterature fascinates the youngsters as they emerge from childhood into early adolescence. But perhaps it might be a more valid approach to ask what needs in the adolescent at this time make him respond so enthusiastically to these books. Most adult readers who take the time to review their own pattern of growing-up-in-reading will recall that they too at one time had a particular affection for exactly this kind of story. The universality of the experience indicates that it is not simply the result of a poor cultural background or an inferior education. To help guide the child to better kinds of books it is essential to understand the basic appeal of these inferior materials.

1. Such material is cheap and easily accessible. Even as adults we tend to read what is at hand rather than make the effort to acquire something more interesting and worthwhile. The child is even more the victim of such casual selection. He picks up the material that is sold in the drugstore, at the newsstand, even in some supermarkets. He browses through the magazines that come regularly into his home. Furthermore, the fact that subliterature generally sells at a cheap or reasonable price is important to the teen-ager. Paperback editions of good literature are providing youngsters with a better level of reading matter at lower cost, but they are not always accessible. Because low cost and ready availability are important factors in teen-age reading, there are paperback book clubs that mail books directly to the students through the schools.

2. Most patterned stories are easy to read. Actually

the reading ease does not lie in a simple vocabulary, short sentences, and uncomplicated ideas. Rather it lies in the fact that each story repeats an old familiar pattern. Once you recognize who are the good guys and who are the bad guys, you can throw yourself into enjoying the intricate, unfolding action. For no matter how impossible the situation may be, the "good guys" will come out on top. With the stereotyped characters and familiar plot patterns, the reader is given definite clues to the outcome.

3. *The story pattern is exactly that of all folk literature.* Folk ballads and folk stories passed on from generation to generation by word of mouth utilize the simplest and most appealing elements of storytelling. The tale moves from one peak of action to another without the sophisticated build-up of information and motive that a more profound writer may use. Folk narrators were seldom worried about the *how* or *why* of their stories. They were only interested in telling *what*. Subliterature follows this same pattern. It too moves from climax to climax with little effort expended on description, characterization, or explanation. Therefore it is not surprising that the young and half-formed reader should respond to exactly the same kind of stories that have always delighted and entertained the unsophisticated common man.

4. *The most important reason for the appeal of subliterature is the high degree of wish fulfillment.* These stories pitch the reader into the kind of life that he secretly yearns to experience for himself but which he seldom can achieve. They are written as if they were actually taking place at this very moment, perhaps in a nearby town. And what lives the characters live! Not the usual humdrum one that most of us face, but a life filled with excitement, challenge, delight, and rewards. The adolescent in real life is hampered by his parents. In the series book, the adolescent is freed of such parental control. Either the parents are presented as being utterly permissive and understanding or they have

conveniently died or gone away on a trip. Furthermore, since the adolescent is convinced that he is far
more perceptive than the adults, inevitably, the adolescent character is the one who solves the baffling
mystery or troubling problem. Naturally the teen-age
protagonists are shown as ingenious, clever, perceptive;
and the adults are pictured as clumsy, inept, bumbling.
The impossible but very real desire of the teen-ager
for high adventure in distant parts of the world is satisfied through the adventure tales. And the young
girl's yearning for romance is fed by the romantic
novels which operate on an unreal plane of emotions
and intensity. Although such situations seldom develop
in actual life, the reader finds the promise of it deeply
satisfying.

Here then are the reasons teen-agers choose this
kind of material: it is inexpensive, accessible, easy to
understand, leaps from crisis to crisis, and shows teen-
agers succeeding in every phase of life. Now granted
that these are not admirable motives, still they are
compelling. And generations of human beings have at
one period of their lives felt the need for the very satisfactions that subliterature provides before they move
on to other kinds of reading.

You need not be concerned if your youngster enjoys this kind of book; but you should be concerned if
he continues to read at this level for an extended time
or if he reads only this kind of material. Still, is there
any actual harm done to the individual if he never
passes beyond this type? All of us know adults who are
still reading nothing but Zane Grey or James Bond.
Obviously they bogged down in their move toward
reading maturity.

The harm in this particular stage of reading is that
such books imply an interpretation of human life that
is unsound if not actually untruthful. For example,
these romantic books imply that life in the country or
the wilds is essentially the good life and life in the city
is inclined to be corrupt and degrading. Frequently

the adolescent heroes are able to do what adults cannot do, whereas the whole accumulated history of
mankind demonstrates that experience and knowledge
bring a wisdom impossible to achieve in a few short
years of living. Subliterature is also filled with racial
and religious stereotypes: the Negro is presented as a
lovable but not very bright servant; the oriental is
crafty and cruel with a childlike sense of humor; anyone belonging to an established Christian church is a
just, kindly, benevolent person. And, character may be
shown by certain physical characteristics. The villain
has, perhaps, a physical deformity or a low brow, a
hawk-shaped nose, clawlike fingers. The heroes and
heroines, on the other hand, are always physically attractive with the best of Anglo-Saxon characteristics.
They may even be tagged with Anglo-Saxon names,
while the villains and their female counterparts are
called by southern European or eastern European
names. Sometimes, clothing is used to indicate the
villain or hero—the former is identified by sloppy, dirty
dress, and the latter by his casual, acceptable clothes.
The good people always win out and gain actual material rewards—job, marriage to the beautiful girl,
gifts of money, cars, scholarships. Finally, differences
in education, background, and culture will vanish if
romantic love is present.

These same false assumptions about human life are
prevalent in other media. They are an integral part of
daily television and radio programs, modern magazine
stories, and even advertising. In other words, certain
assumptions are deeply imbedded in our culture, and
the fact that they appear over and over again makes
it inevitable that these same false beliefs about human
nature will pass on to the next generation. The adult
who accepts these assumptions about life as the truth
will find himself in difficulties when faced with experiences that do not support the assumptions. But the
adult who has learned the facts about human life and
those living it, knows what to expect from his fellow

men and understands that there is a cause-effect principle operating in human relationships.

Because subliterature uniformly presents a false picture of life, it can become harmful to the individual who never passes beyond this stage. The trapped reader never learns to recognize the actual truths of human existence nor gains any depth of understanding for the human beings surrounding him. What attitude, then, should a parent assume when he finds his youngster at this immature reading stage, and how can he move him upward in his reading tastes?

1. Accept the fact that this is a stage in reading which most people experience as they move toward maturity. Do not show by the expression on your face, by your attitude, or by any words that you disapprove. But be alert to see that he does not get stuck at this level of reading.

2. Use satire. After six months or so, joke at the table about the good Anglo-Saxon names of the characters and try to create your own characters to fit these names. Or, make up a story about stereotyped characters in an obviously artificial situation.

3. Point out the stereotypes in other forms of our culture. While watching a television Western you can drop a comment: "Say, that must be the good guy. He's wearing a white hat." Make a game out of identifying the hero by his speech, or physique, or name. When a young person becomes aware of the shallowness of such characterization, he is moving toward maturity in his understanding. Stereotypes in magazine ads can similarly be pointed out by commenting on the fact that such and such a company finally showed a Negro as a doctor instead of as a redcap, or that the rugged cowboy smoking a particular cigarette is probably a New-York dude. In such a game you may even startle yourself by discovering that you too have unwittingly accepted certain false assumptions.

4. So you yourself read Westerns, mysteries, romances. Must you now hide these or give them up so that your child will not be corrupted? The best approach is to point out casually to your adolescent that you read these books with full knowledge of their shallowness, that you realize they are time-fillers but you find in them a release from daily tensions, that you do not take them seriously, and that you would never read only this one kind of book. Point out that you enjoy popcorn or peanuts at times but never as the dominant part of your diet. Subliterature forms the peanuts and popcorn of your reading menu.

5. *Gradually try to find better books that will satisfy your child's needs at this time.* As a parent you need to be informed about the books that may have some of the same basic appeals of the mediocre books but which rise above their level because they avoid gross and erroneous assumptions. If you have a ready supply of books that are exciting and yet well written, you will find that your child is quite perceptive. He will discover on his own how shoddy and false the other materials are. Like you, he may occasionally read one of them for the same reasons you do—to escape the tensions and baffling problems surrounding him. But he will recognize his reason for doing it. In such reading there can be little permanent harm.

Therefore, if you are to be in a position to suggest titles that may appeal to your teen-age reader, you need to know both titles and the kinds of books available for him. If your daughter is reading *Star-Spangled Summer* she is not ready for *Anna Karenina*. This is too great a jump. Nor is your Hardy boy fan ready for *War and Peace*. But between this subliterature and the classics lies a body of material that is respectable literature and yet unknown to the average parent. The next chapter deals with the exciting field of adolescent literature. These books deal with problems, people, and events that hold the young reader's interest; but they are written with a skill and sensitivity not present in sub-reading fare.

Chapter 5
The Adolescent Novel

For everything there is a season, and a time, for every
matter under heaven.

Ecclesiastes 3:1
Revised Standard

In the past thirty years or more the adolescent or
junior novel has been recognized as a distinct type of
literature. These books, written primarily for the young
adult, have the best chance of weaning a teen-ager
between the ages of twelve and fifteen, away from the
subliterature. A primarily American production until
recently, the teen-age novel has often been confused
by adults with the juvenile series books and condemned with them. But teachers and librarians who
are closely associated with the adolescent reader recognize that their most potent tool to help the young
person develop more sophisticated and adult reading
tastes is the adolescent novel. It is an important rung
on the ladder to reading maturity.

What is the adolescent novel? It is a book written by
a serious writer for the teen-age reader. The writer
tries to evoke through his use of words the feelings and
emotions, the triumphs and failures, the tensions and
releases, that people in the age group of twelve to
twenty normally experience. It is not a Sunday School
paper story which sets out to teach moral truths and
incite young people to live the moral life. Actually
many of the better books do not offer any real or con-

vincing solution to the difficulties confronting the characters. Like good adult literature the adolescent novel holds up for the reader's inspection the whole spectrum of human life: the good, the bad; people's successes, their failures; the indifferent, the vicious, the lost. And as in real life there is no neat patterned solution to life's problems.

This kind of book developed slowly. Some of the earliest ones might be termed literary accidents. They were actually written for an adult audience but they were later claimed as his own by the teen-age reader hungry for good books at his own level of interest and ability. Mark Twain's *Huckleberry Finn,* a subtly crafted novel with many possible levels of interpretation, is one of these literary accidents. Louisa May Alcott's *Little Women* was another. Miss Alcott actually wrote this book for an adult audience, but because she showed adolescent girls with a degree of realism never before attempted in American literature, the teen-age girl appropriated it for her own reading. Robert Louis Stevenson's tales of the sea are highly crafted novels which quickly became the property of the boy of twelve or thirteen. In the same way, Jack London's stories of man and nature have appealed to young readers. These books, though not originally intended for the adolescent audience, were enthusiastically read by young readers, thus pointing up the need for material of a respectable literary level answering the needs of the teen-ager. The result has been the modern innovation called "the adolescent novel."

During the average year some three to four hundred such books are published. Some of them are highly stereotyped in plot, devoid of characterization, and dull in their language. But a substantial number each year rise above such mediocrity, and a handful are books of real distinction containing within them the qualities that distinguish literature as great whether it is written for the child, the teen-ager, or the adult audience. The best of each year's crop of adolescent books is slowly building toward a respectable number, making a shelf of distinguished books for the young person to read. Their success may be measured by the length of time they are in print. The good young adult book stays in print for years.

Seventeenth Summer, by Maureen Daly, was published in the early 1940's and is often credited as being the first of the junior novels of distinction and quality. Miss Daly was scarcely more than an adolescent herself when she wrote this book showing adolescent life, not from the adult's viewpoint as he looks back, but rather from the adolescent's viewpoint as he moves through his experiences. This technique is similar to that used in *Huckleberry Finn* and *Little Women*. Her book succeeds because it is an accurate representation of what it feels like to be a seventeen-year-old girl. The story centers on Angie in the summer between her graduation from high school and her enrollment in college and details her first love affair. Because Angie has attended a girls' school, not until her seventeenth summer does she meet Jack, who delivers bakery goods in her small Wisconsin town. The book tells sympathetically of Angie's doubts, her fears, and the unwritten code that governs adolescent behavior. First she is afraid that her family may disgrace her when Jack comes for the initial date, and after he arrives she is afraid that Jack may not measure up to her family's standards. She discovers that her admired older sister has a poor reputation among the boys. And she tastes for the first time the experiences of the dating girl who can join the gang at the drugstore, the beer shack at the lake, the Coke spot . . . all off-limits to the non-dating girl. She is aware of the growing intensity of her feelings for Jack and yet realizes that she still wants to go on to college. When Jack and Angie say their passionate good-byes and vow always to love each other, she instinctively knows that the romance is over and that never again will they be able to recapture the feelings they have at that moment.

At the time this book was published it was unique and represented a whole new approach to the junior novel. Adolescent problems and reactions were taken seriously, just as seriously as they are taken by the young person experiencing them. Furthermore, the book gave a truthful picture of adolescent life. There are beer parties and blanket parties; there is the girl who makes the mistake of dating a boy with a bad reputation; and the sister who attempts to attract boys in all the wrong ways. Today the book seems rather innocent, but at the time it was published many parents and teachers were startled and offended by this frank detailing of adolescent mores and actions.

One of the elements that lifts *Seventeenth Summer* above the ordinary rank of teen-age novels is the subtle understandings Maureen Daly imparts about human relationships. These emerge naturally without any studied preaching. One couple has dated long and faithfully, not because of any real attraction, but because they desperately need the security of each other's attention. Angie's understanding at the end of the book that her romance is a passing thing, that the love she and Jack feel is not strong enough to survive separation, is a far cry from the easy solutions extolled in patterned stories where love conquers all.

The response to *Seventeenth Summer* was immediate and has continued. Probably no book ever captured the imagination of so many adolescent girls so quickly. The English teacher of the forties was inclined to bypass it and continued to concentrate on proclaiming the merits of *Julius Caesar* and *Silas Marner*. But libraries were finding it impossible to keep copies of *Seventeenth Summer* on the shelves. One high school library I visited in these early days of the book had seventy copies on its shelves and yet still had to maintain a waiting list for those who wanted to read or perhaps reread the book. The reaction of the readers was almost unanimous. They loved it. They begged the librarians for more . . . "just as good as this one." But it remained the lone specimen for years. The book is still read widely, but adolescent mores and experiences are changing and so the story is beginning to seem a trifle old-fashioned to the contemporary teen-age girl.

Yet, what today's young reader wants is exactly the same thing in a book that *Seventeenth Summer* had for earlier generations: an honest view of the adolescent world from the adolescent's point of view; a book that holds a mirror up to society today so that the reader can see his own world reflected in it. The adolescent novels of enduring appeal all have these qualities in common. Adolescence is never satirized nor glorified. It is shown as the adolescent himself sees it. The books that are successful with the young reader are generally told from the personal viewpoint of one character rather than in the objective third person. They detail what it feels like to be ashamed of one's parents, to be afraid in a crowd, to be lonely and on the sidelines, to be pushed to the limits of one's physical endurance in a sports event and fail, to enter a contest and be only second best. In other words, the book that is psychologically oriented in its dominant plot line outlives the one that simply tells what happened.

In the past thirty years both the numbers and the merits of the teen-age novel have steadily increased. It is not surprising that these books tend to be classifiable under a dozen or so themes. In addition to stories of boy-girl relationships there are sports stories, science fiction tales, animal stories, books with historical settings, stories of growing up in various cultures around the world, narratives of boys and cars, adventure and mystery tales, vocational stories, and novels with basic moral or ethical dilemmas.

1. Sports Stories: Go, Team, Go! by John Tunis is

typical of the significant sports story. It centers on a basketball team in an Indiana town and has the excitement of the sports contest that is always at the heart of such stories. Some of the games are slow, the players lethargic; others are breath-taking contests that hang on the final throw of the game. Tunis has the ability to evoke the quality of a sport. He makes the reader smell the locker room, feel the desperate fatigue in moments of play, react to the color of a crowd in a gymnasium. Basketball, however, is not really the central theme of the story. *Go, Team, Go!* tells of a team of Juniors who have won the state championship. They are feted by the service clubs of the town, admired by their peers and elders alike. They have become the status figures of both their community and their school. And their coach is the idol of the townspeople. However, one of the quintet, Red, son of the local bookmaker, finds himself in need of money and so he begins a smalltime gambling operation on the school football games. Because of an upset, he is unable to cover his bets and his operation comes to light. He is expelled from the school. In an attempt to pressure the school's administration to readmit Red, the other four members of the team resign. The school authorities stand firm; the coach organizes the second string players into a starting line-up and does nothing to lure the boys back to participating. Almost immediately the community is up in arms and pressures the school officials and the coach to reinstate both Red and the other team members.

As you can see, the story not only presents the actual excitement of the physical contest, but shows the distortion of values that can occur in an American community as the result of this adulation of young high school players. It is a critical book but not a didactic one. Each incident arises out of the characters of the people involved and the nature of the social values under which they live. It leaves the reader to make his own decisions of right and wrong for himself. More and more stories like *Go, Team, Go!* explore the fundamental problems of human relationships and goals. These are, therefore, quite different from the series books centering on sports that many of us read in junior high school, books in which the main concern was the contest itself and the struggle to win the game.

2. *Animal Stories:* Fred Gipson's *Old Yeller* is a fine example of the best of this kind. It is subtly crafted, and the animal-human relationship is merely one thread of an intricately woven fabric of relationships. So popular has Gipson's book been that it has been made into a motion picture and has inspired a TV series. The story deals with Travis, a young boy in the days following the Civil War, who is left in charge of their Texas ranch while his father drives the herd of cattle north for sale. Travis takes his responsibilities seriously and is completely unsympathetic when his little brother drags home a lazy, tricky old hound dog to whom Travis takes an instinctive dislike. Through the story his reactions shift. The climax is reached when Old Yeller staves off the attack of a rabid wolf and is himself bitten by the animal. As a result Travis must shoot him.

As in most families Travis shows little respect for his younger brother, and yet when the youngster is attacked by the wolf, Travis is in a turmoil. Similarly, he has ambiguous feelings towards the dog which he is determined to despise and yet unwillingly comes to like. These conflicts arise because Travis tries to perform a man's job in an adult world and feels that he must hide any affection for his brother or the animal. He is caught between what he thinks a man should feel and what he as a young boy really does feel. The story has action, humor, depth of characterization, and a deftness of language which conveys the very quality of the landscape in the central hill country of Texas.

3. *Stories of Olden Times:* A surprising number of

adolescent novels attempt to evoke life in an earlier period of history. One such classic in this category is *Johnny Tremain*, by Esther Forbes. The author is a scholar who wrote a prize-winning and scholarly adult biography of Paul Revere. Sometime later she brought out the delightful story of Johnny Tremain, an apprentice to a silversmith in the years leading up to the American Revolution. Johnny is a very believable adolescent boy: smart, skillful, self-assured. He dominates the other apprentices until his hand is permanently injured by an accident with molten silver. The reader experiences Johnny's long slow period of recovery, his self-consciousness over his distorted hand, his bitter necessity of finding a new pattern for his life. Eventually he becomes involved in the opening days of the Revolutionary War, and the historical figures he comes to know emerge as living people.

Describing the emotions and reactions of Johnny, Miss Forbes has subtly underscored the idea that human life is basically the same wherever and whenever it is lived. Paul Revere and John Adams are presented as men not unlike people one might know in his own community today. By reading such a book, the young person has the vicarious experience of living in an age different from his own and discovering that the problems of long ago are essentially like the problems that he may face today.

4. Science Fiction: Robert Heinlein's *Farmer in the Sky* is typical of the best in this category. Set in the future, it tells the story of a group of colonists from the Earth who have settled on one of Jupiter's moons, in an environment inhospitable to man's survival. These men must break down rock to make soil, construct sun traps to create tolerable temperatures, import biological specimens from Earth so that cycles of life can be maintained. The book has fascinating scientific speculations and much information. Heinlein is a careful craftsman, and in general his stories are an extension of plausible, scientific and technological information that we possess at the present time. Like the historically oriented book, Heinlein's stories imply the continuity of human strivings—in the future. Although he shows the external conditions of life as changed, the basic feelings, problems, and relationships of people are the same.

In *Farmer in the Sky* family life is similar to family life as we know it today. And by using the pattern of the pioneer story, the author suggests that man is facing a frontier in the future not far different from that which he faced in settling America. One of the distinguishing qualities of Heinlein's writing is the imaginative power displayed. He is able to create fascinating visions of what may exist in other parts of the universe.

5. *Stories of Foreign Cultures:* A significant number of adolescent novels fall in this category. These attempt to show the pattern of life and the quality of life as it is lived in various parts of the world. Generally they deal with an adolescent or a group of adolescents in some intense experience. In recent years some of the best of these books have been written by native authors for their own young people and are available to the American adolescent through translation. For example, *More Than Courage*, by Michel-Aimé Baudouy (translated by Marie Ponsot) is the story of a French boy who is about to flunk out of his school. His parents, who have recently acquired their fortune in postwar industry, insist that their son succeed in the academically oriented private school that he attends. But like the rest of his family the boy is mechanically minded, and to him the courses at school are neither palatable nor comprehensible. When he is forced to stay at home during his vacation period to make up school work, he uses his spare time to rebuild a motorcycle he finds concealed in a shed.

Problems with the young in France are not far different from youth problems in America. The French family

in its desire for status pressures the boy to succeed in
an area for which his abilities do not fit him. The boy's
passion for his motorcycle is similar to that of the
American youngster for his car. Such books are sig-
nificantly different in quality from the stories with
foreign backgrounds turned out for the young readers
in the past. These tended to emphasize the quaint, the
differences in costumes and customs, and gave set
stereotyped characteristics to the foreign individual
instead of presenting him as a real human being.

6. *Boys and Cars:* While books about cars are often
grouped together in one category labeled hot-rod
stories, not all of the cars are hot rods. Sometimes the
car is a real sports car, and sometimes it may be a
classic automobile. Henry Felsen's *Street Rod* is the
story of a boy who buys a beat-up jalopy expressly
against his parents' wishes. The car is the status symbol
of his peers in the small Iowa town in which he lives.
Rick and his friends center their whole lives on their
machines: they talk cars, repair cars, drive cars, love
cars. Felsen describes the prowls around the town
square, the sudden decision to blast off onto country
roads, a hunting trip into a Des Moines park. The
problem presented is not how to prevent boys from
having cars, but how to channel this restless energy
and tremendous mechanical ability into something con-
structive. In the case of *Street Rod,* Rick takes that last
dare to drag, loses control, crashes into a bridge, and
is killed. While most automobile stories do have a certain amount of didacticism, they nevertheless succeed
in capturing and presenting the mysterious, all-con-
suming attachment of a boy for his car. And through
this presentation they do what good literature should
do—help the reader understand himself through the
mirror image of another going through a similar series
of experiences.

7. *Adventure Stories:* Because of old favorites like
Robinson Crusoe, The Swiss Family Robinson, and

Treasure Island, many people instinctively think of the
adventure story when adolescent reading is mentioned.
These books were originally written for an adult audience, but adolescents read them because there was little else published that appealed to their developing
tastes. Generally such stories were about a person who
found himself in a strange and hostile environment
from which he had to escape through his wits and
physical prowess. Today's adventure story is likely to
be more plausible with fewer stereotypes. Yet the high
level of excitement is maintained. For example, Ben
Masselink's *The Danger Islands* centers on Johnny
whose sailing ship is shanghaied by pirates in the
South Pacific. Escaping from the ship which is at sea,
the hero through endurance and skill manages to swim
to a deserted island in the Polynesian group. Bit by
bit, he finds the necessities to maintain life and begins
the arduous process of island-hopping until he finally
reaches one inhabited by a native group. Like *Robinson Crusoe,* the book holds the reader spellbound in
the tense battle for survival. But unlike Defoe's book,
this modern tale contains a great deal of accurate an-
thropological information about the Polynesian peoples
of the Pacific islands.

8. *Mystery Stories:* Closely related to the adventure
story is the mystery story written especially for the
teen-ager. Unlike adult mysteries with murder plots,
the teen-age mystery novel focuses on strange and un-
explained happenings. *Guns in the Heather,* by Lockhart Amerman, describes the experiences of Jonathan
Flower, the son of an American secret-service agent,
when he is lured from his school near Edinburgh by a
false telegram. He is kidnapped, escapes, and then begins the game of cat and mouse . . . sometimes serving
as bait and sometimes as the hunter. He rather quickly
learns that apparently no one is to be trusted. Even
the most innocent situations become a part of the intricate plot to keep the boy and his father apart. And

not until the book nears its end does the reader find
out the reasons for all the mysterious maneuverings. A
youngster reading such stories asks little except to have
his attention held and perhaps be pleasantly frightened. He must be willing to accept implausible situations. But the best of these materials have rapidly
moving plots, interesting and commanding characters,
and a choice of language that gains distinction through
rhythm and color.

9. *Vocational Stories:* This is a type of book that
seldom appears on an adult reading list. It centers
about a particular vocation and its main character is
a young person, recently graduated from high school
or college, who is in the process of entering the job
world. Generally the information about the particular
vocation is accurate, and such information as the
length and kind of training needed, the salaries, the
conditions of work, the patterns for advancement, are
neatly tucked into the story. In most cases these stories
have a strong humanitarian appeal, for the social service aspects of a field are emphasized and the economic
phases are minimized. The best of these books is able
to present its information in a palatable fashion by
concentrating on characters and plot. Stephen Meader's *Snow on Blueberry Mountain* demonstrates what
can be done by a competent author in the field. It is
the story of a farm family whose New England land is
unproductive because of its hilly, rocky, shrub-covered
terrain. The only successful crop is blueberries. The
adolescent boys, unable to go to college, decide to construct a ski run on one of their hills. The problems
are fantastic—the hill has to be cleared of underbrush
and trees, and rocks must be blasted away. Then they
must find money for a ski tow and a shelter house.
Underlying all their difficulties is their vulnerability to
the weather. Meader loads this book with step-by-step
details as the boys meet and solve their problems. He
is careful to use exact prices and the hours of work in-

volved so that the reader has an accurate sense of reality. The undertaking is only modestly successful after many setbacks.

Most young people read a vocational book not so much for the basic facts but for a general picture of an engineer's life, a nurse's, a ballet dancer's, or a doctor's. Here is the real service of such books for their adolescent audience: to detail the frustrations, the satisfactions, the shape of a day's activity . . . in other words, the pattern of life one can anticipate in a particular vocation. Through such reading, the young person may test himself in a similar situation; he may be able to feel whether or not he has the personality or intellectual qualities to succeed in a certain vocation. The best of such books do not hold out the Horatio Alger concept of life—that all will succeed. Rather, they suggest that setbacks are common in any vocation and that only a few reach the top.

10. Stories of Moral or Ethical Dilemmas: A distinguished handful of adolescent novels center on the theme of people's attempts to find a direction for their lives in a world of confusing values. While most of the types of books already described may have some such problem as a part of the story, there are only a few which tie the whole fabric of the plot to such a problem. Often these are some of the best of the junior novels available. Ann Emery in *Sorority Girl* considers the private, exclusive, self-perpetuating clubs that exist in many of the country's larger high schools. So accurately does she describe the situation that each girl who reads the book is sure that Miss Emery has used her school as the model for the story. Jean Burnaby, her heroine, is lured by the external glamor of the Nightingales, who always eat together at the same table in the lunchroom, sit together at the games, cluster together in the halls, chit-chatting. She is thrilled to the "bottom of her toes" when she receives a bid to the group. Bit by bit she drifts apart from her old friends

and then finds herself fearing her sorority sisters' judgment of the boy that she herself finds interesting. She
begins to resent the importance that the group places
on clothes and cars. Jean, like many high school girls
in large schools, questions the values of the close-knit
group. Can you be friends with everyone? Will people
of like interests always flock together? Are the standards of the group the standards of the lowest member
in it? Is the group snobbishness and exclusiveness a
vicious kind of segregation? Faced with the pros and
cons, Jean must decide whether or not she wants to
remain a member of the sorority.

The teen-age novels described in this chapter are
very different from *Tom Swift, Nancy Drew, Hardy
Boys, Tarzan.* Since few adults have actually read this
newer variety, they do not realize that the modern
teen-age novel is as different from the series book as
Gone with the Wind is from a simple romance. The
best of the teen-age books are seriously crafted, written by competent and dedicated writers who use
subtlety in characterization, logical development in
their plot lines, and significant themes that are important to the growing teen-ager. In countless libraries
and classrooms, it is this body of literature that bridges
the gap between children's literature, subliterature,
and serious adult literature. Without them, many a
potential reader would fall into the chasm of non-
reading and never be able to extricate himself.

Bibliography

GIRLS' STORIES

Alcott, Louisa May: *Little Women.* Several editions. In one of
the most famous of all family stories, four sisters—energetic

Jo, kind Meg, proud Amy, and tender Beth—grow up together in early Concord.

Bell, Margaret E.: *Watch for a Tall White Sail.* Morrow, 1948; Tempo. Loneliness and danger characterize life on the Alaskan frontier in the 1880's, but sixteen-year-old Florence also finds romance. The story of her family and her courtship is continued in *The Totem Casts a Shadow* (Morrow, 1949) and *Love Is Forever* (Morrow, 1954).

Benson, Sally: *Junior Miss.* Doubleday, 1941. Sketches about the Graves family, especially sixteen-year-old Lois and fourteen-year-old Judy. Life is never dull with Judy around.

Cavanna, Betty: *Going on Sixteen.* Westminster, 1946. Julie is shy and withdrawn, but she learns that by sharing her talents and interests with others she can make friends and understand herself better.

Cleary, Beverly: *Jean and Johnny.* Morrow, 1959. Jean is infatuated with a handsome, popular senior, but learns that infatuation is not the same as love.

Craig, Margaret M.: *Three Who Met.* Crowell, 1959. Three very different girls meet at a house party, where they share a room and learn from each other's experiences during their short time together.

Daly, Maureen: *Seventeenth Summer.* Dodd, 1948. Angie Morrow, who has gone to a girls' school and never dated, meets and falls in love with Jack Duluth in her last summer before going away to college.

Emery, Anne: *The Popular Crowd.* Westminster, 1961. Sue learns the costs of popularity and the value of friendship.

Frank, Anne: *The Diary of a Young Girl.* Doubleday, 1952; Pocket. Anne Frank records the impressions of a young girl growing up amid the tension of two families living together in hiding during the Nazi occupation of Amsterdam.

George, Jean: *Summer of the Falcon.* Criterion, 1962. A girl and her sparrow hawk grow wiser and stronger through three summers together.

Medearis, Mary: *Big Doc's Girl.* Lippincott, 1950; Pyramid. The death of her father, a respected doctor in the Arkansas backwoods, changes Mary's plans for the future and influences her choice of a career and a suitor.

Stolz, Mary: *Ready or Not.* Harper, 1953; Perennial. A New York girl in an East River housing development accepts responsibility as housekeeper for her family after the death of her mother.

————: *To Tell Your Love.* Harper, 1950. While Anne Arma-
cost is recovering from an unhappy first love, her older
sister is enjoying a sudden but stable courtship.

————: *Who Wants Music on Monday.* Harper, 1963. Cassie
Dunne is an individualist with a clear sense of values in
a family of conformists. Her flighty, boy-crazy younger
sister is only one of her problems.

West, Jessamyn: *Cress Delahanty.* Harcourt, 1953; Pocket.
Beautifully written series of story sketches about adolescent life on a California ranch.

York, Carol: *Sparrow Lake.* Coward, 1962. Lydia's friendship
with a boy from the wrong side of the tracks is developing
shyly into love until her sophisticated aunt sends her off
to boarding school.

SPORTS

Allison, Bob, and Frank E. Hill: *The Kid Who Batted 1,000.*
Doubleday, 1951. A lively and humorous story of an Oklahoma youth who can hit any ball thrown.

Archibald, Joe: *Quarterback and Son.* Macrae, 1964. Steve
Logan discovers that his father is using him to gain vicarious success and revenge on the football field.

Frick, C. H.: *Patch.* Harcourt, 1957. A miler who runs just for
fun has to learn teamwork and concentration; but his
teammates and the fans have a lot to learn from him about
the sheer joy of the sport.

Friendlich, Dick: *All-Pro Quarterback.* Westminster, 1963.
After a disappointing second place finish, the Prospectors
trade their first-string quarterback, Chris Blades, to the
Rangers. With them he starts his career all over again.

————: *Full-Court Press.* Westminster, 1962. The community
makes life hard for a young, inexperienced basketball
coach, but he proves himself before the season is over.

Gault, William C.: *The Long Green.* Dutton, 1965. The career
of a golfer is traced from the time he is a caddy, through
high school and college, until he makes it as a pro.

Harkins, Philip: *No Head for Soccer.* Morrow, 1964. A new
country and a new sport call for many adjustments from
Tony, who in his senior year exchanges football at Hill-
crest High for soccer at the Château du Lac.

Heuman, William: *Powerhouse Five.* Dodd, 1963. The world
of industrial basketball is the background in which a young

college graduate must win his place among men that resent his being hired to coach them.

Hutto, Nelson A.: *Breakaway Back*. Harper, 1963. Suspicions of illegal recruitment are directed at Scotty when he transfers to a larger high school for the vocational training he wants.

Tunis, John: *All-American*. Harcourt, 1942. A talented football player transfers from a private academy to a public high school and finds that there are many kinds of prejudice in the community as well as in the school.

———: *Go, Team, Go!* Morrow, 1954. When the whole first string of the state championship basketball team quits in protest, Hooks Barnum holds out against community pressure and builds a new team from scratch.

———: *Yea! Wildcats!* Harcourt, 1944. Don Henderson loses his job as coach because he refuses to be a party to shady recruiting tactics. His fight for fair play and community improvement is continued in *A City for Lincoln*.

ANIMALS

Adair, Margaret: *Far Voice Calling*. Doubleday, 1964; Tempo. Toivo Jarvenin, a lonely boy living in Oregon with his bitter Finnish uncle, rescues a baby sea lion, rears it, and eventually lets it return to the sea.

Bagnold, Enid: *National Velvet*. Morrow, 1949; Grosset; Tempo. With a horse that she wins in a village lottery, Velvet goes on the Grand National Steeplechase.

Burnford, Sheila: *The Incredible Journey*. Little, Brown, 1961; Bantam. A Labrador retriever, a Siamese cat, and an old English bull terrier make a perilous 250-mile trek across a Canadian forest.

Clark, Billy C.: *Good-Bye, Kate*. Putnam, 1965. Kate is a Kentucky mule with a mind of her own, and the boy Isaac hardly knows whether he's her master or her servant.

Farley, Walter: *Black Stallion*. Random, 1941; Perennial. A boy and a stallion, the only survivors of a shipwreck, are rescued from their desolate island and go on to racing fame. The first and best known of a series of books.

Gipson, Fred: *Old Yeller*. Harper, 1956; Perennial. With the help of an exasperating but incredibly intelligent old dog, Travis takes care of his family while his father is on a cattle drive.

James, Will: *Smoky the Cow Horse.* Scribners, 1926; Bantam. The training, work, and mistreatment of a cow pony on the range are described in colorful cowboy language and authentic detail.

Kjelgaard, Jim: *Big Red.* Holiday, 1956. The first of several stories about a champion Irish setter and a trapper's son in the Canadian wilderness. Together they conquer blizzards, varmints, and a great outlaw bear.

Knight, Eric: *Lassie Come Home.* Holt, 1940; Tempo. In this famous dog story, Lassie returns from Scotland hundreds of miles to her young master from whom she has been carried away.

London, Jack: *The Call of the Wild.* Several editions. The survival of the strongest is the theme of this story of Buck, the sledge dog in the Klondike who escapes service to return to the wild.

Murphy, Robert: *The Pond.* Dutton, 1964; Avon. From the time of his first hunting and fishing trip, Joey's understanding of the woods, the animals, and several eccentric men increases.

North, Sterling: *Rascal.* Dutton, 1963; Avon. The author tells of a pet he owned during his boyhood in rural Wisconsin around 1918.

O'Hara, Mary: *Green Grass of Wyoming.* Lippincott, 1946. Ken McLaughlin grows up, learning about horses and himself, on a ranch in Wyoming. Two earlier books about the same family are *My Friend Flicka* (Lippincott, 1941) and *Thunderhead* (Lippincott, 1943).

Rawlings, Marjorie Kinnan: *The Yearling.* Scribners, 1938; Scribners, 1941, 1947, 1961. Jody and his pet fawn grow to maturity together in the Florida Everglades.

Shaefer, Jack: *Old Ramon.* Harcourt, 1963; Bantam. An old sheepherder and an old dog teach a young boy and a young dog about the hard facts of life.

Street, James: *Goodbye, My Lady.* Lippincott, 1954. Skeeter, who lives in the Mississippi swamps with his illiterate Uncle Jesse, discovers, captures, and trains a strange and valuable dog.

STORIES OF OLDEN TIMES

Arnold, Elliott: *Broken Arrow*. Meredith, 1954. Even the blood-
brother relationship of Cochise and Tom Jeffords could
not prevent the last of the Great Indian Wars.

Behn, Harry: *The Faraway Lurs*. World Pub., 1963. In this
Romeo and Juliet kind of story with a prehistoric setting,
a boy and girl of enemy tribes fall in love and are sacri-
ficed because of the hatred of their people.

Catton, Bruce: *Banners at Shenandoah*. Doubleday, 1955; Bantam. A novel by the Pulitzer prize winning author about
a young boy who rides with the Union cavalry.

Caudill, Rebecca: *The Far-Off Land*. Viking, 1964. On a flat-
boat headed for Tennessee, young Ketty learns to accept
discomfort and fear, but because of her Moravian training
cannot reconcile herself to the hatred of the Indians.

Emery, Anne: *Spy in Old Detroit*. Rand McNally, 1963. During the siege of Fort Detroit, Paul Girard's loyalty is torn
between Frenchmen like his brother Philippe and English-
men like his friend John Rutherford.

Fast, Howard: *April Morning*. Crown, 1961; Bantam. Adam
Cooper grows to manhood in one dramatic day—the first
day of the American Revolution. He becomes the man of
the family when his father is killed by the Redcoats on
the town common.

Forbes, Esther: *Johnny Tremain*. Houghton, 1943; Riverside.
Johnny is an arrogant apprentice to a silversmith in pre-
Revolutionary Boston until he burns his hand in an accident. Then he becomes a messenger boy and sees the
political intrigue and preparations for war. Newbery Award
winner.

Hunt, Irene: *Across Five Aprils*. Follett, 1964; Tempo. Jethro,
living on a southern Illinois farm during the Civil War,
is intensely loyal to the Union, but also loves his Rebel
brother and sympathizes with his friend who is a deserter.

Keith, Harold: *Komantcia*. Crowell, 1965. A fifteen-year-old
Spanish aristocrat suffers from the cruelty of his Comanche
Indian captors. Though he admires their courage and
eventually finds friends among them, he never accepts
their ways.

————: *Rifles for Watie*. Crowell, 1957. A Union soldier sees
both sides of the war when he is befriended by the Rebel

soldiers upon whom he is spying and witnesses the treach-
ery of his own commanding officer. Newbery Award
winner.

Malvern, Gladys: *The Foreigner.* McKay, 1956. This skillful
retelling of the biblical story of Naomi and Ruth is enriched by a wealth of geographical and social detail.

Pease, Howard: *Thunderbolt House.* Doubleday, 1944. A mysterious house in San Francisco represents wealth to a
family which moves there just before the great earthquake
and fire.

Speare, Elizabeth George: *The Bronze Bow.* Houghton, 1961.
Daniel is as obsessed with hatred for the Romans and
desire for vengeance as his sister Leah is with the "de-
mons" of fear, until he meets a rabbi named Jesus. Newbery Award winner.

————: *The Witch of Blackbird Pond.* Houghton, 1958. When
Kit Tyler comes from the Barbados to live with her Puritan relatives in colonial Connecticut, she is not prepared
to accept the austere life of hard work—nor to stand accused as a witch! Newbery Award winner.

SCIENCE FICTION

Bradbury, Ray: *R Is for Rocket.* Doubleday, 1965. Bantam.
Tales of terror and adventure, including the space-age
classic, "Frost and Fire."

Clarke, Arthur C.: *Dolphin Island.* Holt, 1963. In an exciting
sea adventure of the future, Johnny struggles with a killer
whale and a typhoon, and attempts to communicate with
the dolphins.

Del Rey, Lester: *Outpost of Jupiter.* Holt, 1963. The health
and longevity of the colonists on Ganymede are threatened by a dangerous plague until the alien creatures from
Jupiter come to their aid.

Heinlein, Robert A.: *Farmer in the Sky.* Scribners, 1950; Avon.
The dangers and anxieties of frontier life in outer space
force Bill and his dad to make many adjustments.

————: *Podkayne of Mars.* Putnam, 1963; Avon. Science fiction
for girls. A sixteen-year-old descendant of Earthmen living on Mars becomes involved in political intrigue.

————: *The Rolling Stones.* Scribners, 1962. A restless space
family buys a used rocket from Dealer Dan, the Spaceship
Man, and are off on an interplanetary vacation.

L'Engle, Madeleine: *A Wrinkle in Time*. Farrar, Straus, 1962. Meg and her companions tesseract through time in search of her missing scientist father. A scientific fantasy with overtones of allegory. Newbery Award winner.

Norton, André: *Key out of Time*. World Pub., 1963; Ace. Two agents sent back 10,000 years in time become involved in a feud between the mechanized Rovers and a strange occult civilization.

————: *The X-Factor*. World Pub., 1965. Mental telepathy opens up a means of communication between brothers-in-fur and brothers-in-flesh and helps a young man find a useful place in his universe.

Nourse, Alan E.: *Star Surgeon*. McKay, 1959. Dal Timgar, a young physician from the planet Garv, encounters prejudice, self-doubt, and the problems of a very trying first flight to win his place in interplanetary medicine.

————: *The Universe Between*. McKay, 1965. The Threshold universe offers a route to an infinity of universes. Robert Benedict faces the challenge and panic of life in another dimension.

Verne, Jules: *Twenty Thousand Leagues Under the Sea*. Several editions. First published in 1869, this account of Captain Nemo's *Nautilus* sounds strangely like that of a modern submarine.

FOREIGN CULTURES

Baudouy, Michel-Aimé: *More Than Courage*. Harcourt, 1961. A French boy whose parents are displeased with his poor grades and his choice of friends wins self-confidence and his father's respect.

Benary-Isbert, Margot: *The Ark*. Harcourt, 1953. A German family just after the Second World War finally finds a new home in an abandoned streetcar.

————: *Rowan Farm*. Harcourt, 1954. In this sequel to *The Ark*, Margret must choose between an easier life in America and staying with her family at Rowan Farm where she is needed.

Bennett, Jack: *Jamie*. Little, Brown, 1963; Bantam. A white boy growing up in South Africa vows to shoot the wild buffalo that killed his father.

Bishop, Claire Huchet: *The Big Loop*. Viking, 1955. Bicycle racing, a national sport in France, brings excitement and honor to André Girard, a neglected Paris boy.

Clark, Ann Nolan: *Santiago*. Viking, 1955. Santiago's adventures take him into all levels of Guatemalan life—from the luxury of the Spanish aristocrats to the deprivation of a primitive Indian village.

Forman, James: *Ring the Judas Bell*. Farrar, Straus, 1965. Nicholos and his cynical sister are among the 30,000 children kidnaped by the Communist Andarté in Greece after the Second World War.

Fukei, Arlene: *East to Freedom*. Westminster, 1964. The approach of the Communists in northern China in 1948 brings a series of crises for Mei-lin, a schoolgirl, and her fiancé, Ling-wen.

Guillot, René: *Fofana*. Criterion, 1962. The friendship between the French boy, Jean-Luc, and the native African boy, Fofana, brings together two different cultures and two views of life.

Hahn, Emily: *Francie*. Grosset, 1954; Tempo. At first Francie doesn't like the idea of living in England during her last year of high school; but as she and the English students get to know each other better, their attitudes change.

Hogarth, Grace Allen: *As a May Morning*. Harcourt, 1958. An English schoolgirl is so excited about her correspondence with an American boy and her dream of studying in the United States that she neglects her studies.

Holm, Ann: *North to Freedom*. Harcourt, 1965. A dramatic story about a young boy who escapes from a concentration camp and has to learn the most elementary things about the world outside.

Knight, Ruth A.: *First the Lightning*. Doubleday, 1955. An Italian boy is tempted to join in a street gang in order to get enough money for his mother and himself to survive.

Lewis, Elizabeth Foreman: *To Beat a Tiger*. Holt, 1956. Sixteen boys from all levels of society form a street gang and live by their cunning, courage, and loyalty to each other during the Japanese occupation of Shanghai.

Morris, Edita: *Flowers of Hiroshima*. Viking, 1959; Pocket. A grimly realistic picture of the suffering in Hiroshima fourteen years after the time of the bomb. A sympathetic American sees, but can't understand, its mark on one family.

Seuberlich, Hertha: *Annuzza, a Girl of Romania*. Rand McNally, 1962. In boarding school, Annuzza had dreamed of an elegant family estate, but back in her own village she finds her place teaching in the peasant school.

Sherman, D. R.: *Old Mali and the Boy*. Little, Brown, 1964. Fatherless Jeff, living in India, has learned to depend on the aged gardner, Mali, who gives him a prized bow and arrows and takes him on his first big hunting trip.

Somerfelt, Aimee: *Miriam*. Criterion, 1962; Scholastic. Miriam lives through the violent anti-Semitism of Nazi-occupied Norway; the cruelty, loss, and danger are made bearable only by the loyalty of a handful of friends.

Thorvall, Kerstin: *Girl in April*. Harcourt, 1963. A small-town Swedish girl goes to Stockholm to attend a design school.

Wojciechowska, Maia: *Shadow of a Bull*. Atheneum, 1964. The son of Spain's greatest bullfighter believes he has no choice but to follow in his legendary father's footsteps in a life for which he realizes he is not suited. Newbery Award winner.

CARS

Carter, Bruce: *Speed Six*. Harper, 1956. The 24-hour race at Le Mans is always a challenge, but especially so when the car is a 25-year-old Speed Six Bentley.

Castex, Pierre: *Nightmare Rally*. Abelard, 1965. A young garage mechanic rebuilds a wrecked Renault Dauphine to compete in the Brie Rally, but gets involved in a mystery even more exciting than the race.

Felsen, Henry Gregor: *Boy Gets Car*. Random, 1960. To his astonishment, Woody finds that instead of possessing a car he is being possessed by it, to the detriment of his grades, finances, and disposition.

————: *Hot Rod*. Dutton, 1950; Bantam. Bud Crayne's recklessness and cynical bravado make him a hero for a while, but eventually lead to tragedy.

————: *Street Rod*. Random, 1953; Bantam. Ricky's adventures in a hot-rod gang and later in a state-wide auto design contest lead to an unexpected conclusion.

Gault, William C.: *Dirt Track Summer*. Dutton, 1961. The two sons of a great auto racing mechanic take to the dirt track circuit against their father's wishes.

Harkins, Philip: *The Day of the Drag Race*. Morrow, 1960; Berkley. The choice between a career in automobile rac-

ing and a college education is not as easy to make as
Oscar had expected.

————: *Road Race*. Crowell, 1953; Scholastic. Though David's
initiation stunt in the local hot rod club leads to his arrest,
later he and the club learn the value of genuine skill and
knowledge in handling cars.

Jackson, C. Paul: *Super-Modified Driver*. Hastings, 1964. The
son of a famous retired driver starts his racing career by
building and testing his own car.

Jones, Evan, ed.: *High Gear*. Bantam, 1955. A collection of
stories about racing cars and their drivers, by famous
authors.

Olson, Gene: *Bailey and the Bearcat*. Westminster, 1964. The
use of antique automobiles as a publicity stunt in a small
California town brings about a series of hilarious incidents.

Stanford, Don: *The Red Car*. Funk & Wagnalls, 1954; Scholastic; Tempo. Hap spends the summer working to pay for
and rebuild a wrecked red MG, then tests it and himself
in a local road race.

ADVENTURE STORIES

Annixter, Paul: *Swiftwater*. Hill & Wang, 1951; Riverside.
Bucky takes over his injured father's place as hunter and
trapper and shares his dream of a sanctuary for the wild
geese.

Bonham, Frank: *Burma Rifles*. Crowell, 1960; Berkley. In spite
of the outrageous treatment of Japanese-Americans in re-
location camps after Pearl Harbor, Jerry Harada and his
Nisei companions prove their loyalty and heroism with
Merrill's Marauders.

Clarke, Tom E.: *The Big Road*. Lothrop, 1963. Vic Martin
drops out of school and becomes a teen-age hobo during
the Depression of the 30's. Based on the author's actual
experiences.

Gipson, Fred: *Savage Sam*. Harper, 1962; Pocket. The son of
Old Yeller pursues a band of Apaches who have captured
and tormented Travis, Little Arliss, and Lisbeth.

Goldthwaite, Priscilla: *Night of the Wall*. Putnam, 1964. On
the first night of the Berlin Wall, Hans's mother is imprisoned in East Berlin for smuggling medicine to the
underground.

Jefferis, Barbara: *Solo for Several Players*. Sloane, 1961. Janet

Osbourne cannot pilot a plane and even fears flying, but a freak accident puts her alone in an airborne craft over Australia.

Kipling, Rudyard: *Captains Courageous*. Several editions. Harvey, the spoiled son of a millionaire, is rescued by a fishing schooner off the Newfoundland banks and forced to live and work with its crew.

Masselink, Ben: *The Danger Islands*. Little, Brown, 1964. Alone on uninhabited Polynesian islands, Johnny experiences an exciting Robinson Crusoe kind of adventure.

O'Dell, Scott: *Island of the Blue Dolphins*. Houghton, 1960. An Indian girl, left by her tribe, survives alone for eighteen years on a bleak island off the coast of California. Based on an actual experience. Newbery Award winner.

Pease, Howard: *Shipwreck*. Doubleday, 1957. Renny was warned not to sail on the *Samarang*, but it was his only chance to find out about the mysterious disappearance of his father's schooner on the Tanga Sea.

Phleger, Marjorie: *Pilot Down, Presumed Dead*. Harper, 1963. The survivor of a crash landing struggles to stay alive on an uninhabited island off the coast of Baja California with a coyote for his only companion.

Senje, Sigurd: *Escape!* Harcourt, 1964. Aided by two young Norwegians and a crafty telegraph operator, a prisoner of war escapes from a Nazi prison camp.

Tunis, John: *Silence over Dunkerque*. Morrow, 1962; Berkley. A British sergeant retreating from France in 1940 makes it back to England only because of the ingenuity and courage of a young French girl.

Ullman, James Ramsey: *Banner in the Sky*. Lippincott, 1954. Rudi is determined to conquer the Citadel, the treacherous mountain his father died trying to climb. Many descriptive details are based on the actual ascent of the Matterhorn.

Werstein, Irving: *The Long Escape*. Scribners, 1964. After Hitler's invasion of Belgium, Justine Raymond flees to England with fifty convalescent children.

MYSTERIES

Amerman, Lockhart: *Cape Cod Casket*. Harcourt, 1964. Jonathan Flower and his secret agent father become involved with the weird Dr. Sarx, a mad embalmer, and his colleague, a Parsi priest.

————: *Guns in the Heather*. Harcourt, 1963. When Jonathan
leaves his Scottish boarding school, he stumbles into international intrigue in which he can't tell his friends from
his enemies.

Holt, Victoria: *Bride of Pendorric*. Doubleday, 1963; Crest.
An ominous superstition about the brides of Pendorric confronts the latest bride when her husband brings her to
his dark old English castle.

L'Engle, Madeleine: *The Arm of the Starfish*. Farrar, Straus,
1965. A young marine biologist on his way to an assignment in Portugal is warned of some suspicious characters
on his plane.

Park, Ruth: *Secret of the Maori Cave*. Doubleday, 1964. Mystery and anthropology are the components of adventure
for a family which has come to the brush country of New
Zealand to sell some property left them by an eccentric
uncle.

Stevenson, Robert Louis: *Kidnapped*. Several editions. Scotland in the time of the Jacobite uprising of 1745 is the
scene for this popular adventure story.

————: *Treasure Island*. Several editions. Long John Silver
and his notorious companions are frighteningly alive in
this tale of pirates, hidden treasure, and a boy's secret.

Thum, Marcella: *Mystery at Crane's Landing*. Dodd, 1964.
Strange things happen to the Crane family during the
celebration of the Civil War centennial in their small
Southern town.

Westreich, Budd: *The Day It Rained Sidneys*. McKay, 1965.
An American youth on his first trip abroad expects to be
met in London by his friend Sidney, but instead meets
two Sidneys and learns from a third man that Sidney is
dead!

Whitney, Phyllis: *Black Amber*. Meredith, 1964; Crest. An
attractive American girl in Istanbul becomes involved in-
directly in illegal narcotic traffic.

————: *Secret of the Emerald Star*. Westminster, 1964. A
blind Cuban girl's mysterious emerald and diamond pin
leads Robin Ward to excitement and to a better understanding of human nature.

VOCATIONS

Archibald, Joe: *Jet Flier*. McKay, 1960. A commercial airline pilot contemplating an emergency landing looks back over his whole flying career.

Atwater, Montgomery: *Avalanche Patrol*. Random, 1951. Excitement and adventure are part of a day's work for a snow ranger in the forest service who patrols a dangerous ski resort.

————: *Hank Winton, Forest Ranger*. Random, 1947. A young forest ranger goes through training and faces his first assignment. A sequel is *Hank Winton, Smokechaser* (Random, 1947).

Baner, Skuldav: *First Parting*. McKay, 1960. After a year as teacher of the one-room school in desolate Clay, North Dakota, leaving is almost as hard for Anna Magnuson as coming had been.

George, Jean: *Gull Number 737*. Crowell, 1964. Luke overcomes his resentment and learns to appreciate the painstaking work of his scientist father.

Harris, Christie: *You Have To Draw a Line Somewhere*. Atheneum, 1964; Tempo. The author's daughter combines her career as a New York fashion designer with a satisfying personal life.

Hentoff, Nat: *Jazz Country*. Harper, 1965. A white boy finds how difficult it is to make good as a jazz musician in Harlem and sees race relations from a different viewpoint.

Meader, Stephen: *Bulldozer*. Harcourt, 1951; Voyager. The step-by-step details, as Bill Crance builds his earth-moving business, are as exciting as the perilous adventures it involves him in.

————: *Snow on Blueberry Mountain*. Harcourt, 1961. A high school boy establishes a ski-slope business to help provide for his family, but finds time for basketball, schoolwork, and an attractive girl.

Newell, Hope: *A Cap for Mary Ellis*. Harper, 1958. Mary and Julie face the same problems faced by student nurses everywhere, and also those that arise because they are the first Negroes to be admitted to the school. A sequel is *Mary Ellis, Student Nurse* (Harper, 1958).

Russell, Sheila: *A Lamp Is Heavy*. Lippincott, 1950. A realistic portrayal of what it's like to become a nurse.

72

THE ADOLESCENT NOVEL

Woody, Regina: *Student Dancer*. Houghton, 1951. Written by a former ballerina, this account of a girl's first year in a New York school of the dance introduces real dancers and teachers.

MORAL AND ETHICAL PROBLEMS

Benary-Isbert, Margot: *The Long Way Home*. Harcourt, 1959. The problems of adjustment to American life by modern immigrants is dramatized in the experiences of a young refugee from East Germany and his friends.

Bennett, Eve: *A Walk in the Moonlight*. Messner, 1959; Nova. A girl has difficulty facing the future after her reputation is shattered by malicious gossip.

Bonham, Frank: *Durango Street*. Dutton, 1965. A story of young gangs told from the point of view of Rufus, a Negro probationer.

Bragdon, Elspeth. *There Is a Tide*. Viking, 1964. When he goes to the island retreat with his father, Nat thinks of himself as already a failure at fifteen, having been kicked out of one too many schools.

Carson, John F.: *The 23rd Street Crusaders*. Farrar, Straus, 1958. A skillful coach turns a neighborhood gang into a polished basketball team, and at the same time saves his own career, marriage, and self-respect.

Emery, Anne: *Sorority Girl*. Westminster, 1952. The Nightingale Sorority affords more problems than answers for disillusioned Jean Burnaby.

Eyerly, Jeannette: *Drop-Out*. Lippincott, 1963. To escape dismal family situations, a young couple leave school and elope, but they find that they are not mature enough to face the crises that immediately arise.

Felsen, Henry Gregor: *Two and the Town*. Scribners, 1964; Scribners. In this frank but sensitively told story the town's football hero and a shy girl he has dated only once are forced into marriage because she is going to have his child. He is too bitter and resentful to accept family responsibility.

Johnson, Annabel and Edgar Johnson: *Pickpocket Run*. Harper, 1961. A young man who needs money to begin life on his own refuses to take part in a scheme of petty robbery.

L'Engle, Madeleine: *Camilla*. Crowell, 1965. A fifteen-year-old daughter of wealthy but unstable parents comes to a realistic understanding of the social and psychological problems of her world, the needs of her friends, and her own capacity for love.

Means, Florence: *It Takes All Kinds*. Houghton, 1964. Unemployment, poverty, and mental retardation are all problems in the Cochran family, but Florrie is sensible, hard-working, and determined to make the best of their life.

————: *Tolliver*. Houghton, 1963. After her graduation from Fisk University, Tolly is swept into the struggle for human rights when she accompanies her younger sister on a Freedom Ride.

Pease, Howard: *Dark Adventure*. Doubleday, 1950. While he is suffering from amnesia, Johnnie Stevens becomes a wanderer on the fringe of society, among hoboes, and would-be dope peddlers.

Riter, Dorris: *Edge of Violence*. McKay, 1964. On a year's probation from a juvenile home, Dirk only slowly recovers from the bitterness of his past and adjusts to family life.

Stolz, Mary: *A Love or a Season*. Harper, 1964; Tempo. Harry, a disturbed and slightly rebellious boy, and Nan, the girl next door, fall in love—or think they fall in love—in a wonderful but nearly disastrous summer.

————: *Rosemary*. Harper, 1955. A working girl in a college town cannot afford to go to college herself and envies those who can. She is influenced by a sociology student who boards in her home.

Summers, James L.: *The Limit of Love*. Westminster, 1959. Lee Hansen, a young college student, has been dating Ronnie since high school days. When she thinks she is pregnant, he can't face what he thinks is his ruined future.

Whitney, Phyllis: *Willow Hill*. McKay, 1947. High school students find a way to solve the conflict that arises when Negro factory workers move into the previously all-white community.

Wier, Ester: *The Loner*. McKay, 1963. A nameless abandoned boy suffers the harshness of a migrant worker's life until he finds a stopping-place on a Montana sheep ranch.

Chapter 6
The Popular Adult Book

For it is impossible that anything should be universally
tasted and approved by the multitude, though they are
only the rabble of the nation, which hath not in it some
peculiar aptness to please and gratify the mind of man.

Addison

Most adolescents will move into the reading of truly
adult literature through the medium of the popular
contemporary novel. It is rather difficult to predict
the age at which the young reader will become dis-
satisfied with the adolescent story written especially
for him. Some young people will begin to feel insulted
by the material as early as the eighth or ninth grade,
and others may still enjoy the adolescent novel as late
as the senior year in high school. Probably the average
age for the change is fifteen or sixteen when the child
is in the tenth grade.

Often the change will be as dramatic as the child's
discovery that the girls' and boys' departments no
longer have clothing suitable for him and that he must
move into a new store or new department to make his
purchases. Growth in reading patterns is not unlike the
changes that the child undergoes in his clothing needs.
The time comes when the young adult begins to feel
that the junior novel is a bit condescending, pat and
stereotyped in plot, obviously centered on young people his own age, and simplified in language. He may
still have a fairly distorted vision of adulthood, but he
wants books that give him the feeling that he is at last
really reading about the adult world.

A small, rather distinguished handful of books are transition literature between the junior novel and the truly adult novel and yet do not fit neatly into either category. These books tend to be more mature in tone, much more mature in the experiences they detail, and yet in general are read exclusively by the teen-age reader. Marguerite Bro's *Sarah*, for example, has all of the appearance of an adult book. It is reasonably long and basically more complex than most junior novels. Sarah is a teen-ager with two real talents: one in music and one in art. Because of a promise made to her dying father she finds herself pursuing the field that is less interesting to her. Thus, we have a character in the throes of a value decision. The novel follows Sarah into young adult life where her world collapses with the death of her fiancé. But after a period, she finds that she is still alive and that it is possible to fall in love a second time.

Maggie, by Vivian Breck, is another transitional book. Although it deals with a young adult's life, it is not quite an adult novel. Maggie, the pampered daughter of a wealthy San Francisco family, falls in love and marries a young engineer working on a project in a Mexican village. The change in environment very nearly ends the marriage as Maggie starts to wonder whether love is enough.

For boys, the war stories of Robb White serve a similar transition function. *Up Periscope* or *Torpedo Run* have the realism, the toughness, the psychological involvement of the adult war story, but they are shorter, easier to read and they minimize sex experiences. Still, the young male reader feels that he is getting something with considerably more guts than he found in teen-age sports books.

Beyond this group of transition stories we come to the popular adult book. This is the kind of book that is read widely and discussed casually. It usually makes the best seller lists and often is selected by one of the

major book clubs. The story may eventually be used as
the basis of a motion picture. And yet within a few
years it fades into oblivion. It does not become a part
of the continuing literary heritage that people cherish
generation after generation.

This kind of book usually tells a gripping story and
it may succeed in creating a character that captures
the imagination of the general public. Thus a book like
Exodus has enormous appeal because of its dramatic
story line, while *Rebecca*, by Daphne Du Maurier,
captivated readers by its picture of a selfish, beautiful,
arrogant woman, unbelievable in many ways, yet utterly fascinating. However, most popular adult books
lack two other qualities found in really great literature:
a significant and enduring theme and a sensitivity to
the flow of language. The popular adult book may
hold the individual spellbound as he reads, but once
finished, he finds that nothing significant has been said
or that the message is stereotyped and commonplace.
Usually missing completely from the popular adult
book is that strange, moving quality that language can
take on in the hands of the great writer. On first reading the excitement of the popular story carries the
reader along. But on rereading, the language seems
quite flat or even insipid. To sense the difference, try
reading the material by two different writers treating
the same scene. Compare, for example, the description
of Christ's entry into Jerusalem as Sholem Asch presents it in *The Nazarene* with Lloyd C. Douglas' description in *The Robe*. One can feel the difference
between the great writing of Asch and the popular
writing of Douglas.

Nevertheless, these popular books fill most of the
leisure time of the reading public. These are the books
that they will continue to read for the rest of their
lives. And rightly so, for they are the expression of
contemporary cultural life. Many adolescent readers

will never grow beyond them, but they should achieve at least this level of sophistication in their reading.

The adult story that appeals to a young girl usually has a girl or a woman as the leading character—especially a woman of great strength of character with a commanding personality like Scarlet O'Hara in *Gone with the Wind.* Girls most thoroughly enjoy books in which the woman heroine is really important to the ongoing life around her. Thus the character may be a young person in the process of finding direction for herself or she may be an older person on whom others depend.

One type of book that appeals to girls is the romance. Romance as a type does not imply simply a love story, although this is almost always a part of it. Such books present a picture of life in which there is a certain quality of hidden mystery and a heightening of emotional response. Life in these romances seems to be slightly unreal like the scenes in a tapestry. One of the favorite writers of this kind of story is Mary Stewart, who has turned out a whole series of books. Each is set in a strangely fascinating part of Europe— the Greek islands, the Austrian Alps—and each centers on an essentially nice but spirited English girl who finds herself involved in a haunting series of mysterious happenings and in a love affair. The heroine always takes risks and moves towards danger relentlessly with a kind of feminine James Bond determination. Part of the great charm of the Stewart books lies in the historical information Miss Stewart imparts and the quality of landscape in her settings. In *Airs Above the Ground,* for example, she laces the book with a great deal of fascinating information about the Lipizzaner horses, while in *This Rough Magic* she weaves in the details that have led people to choose Corfu as the legendary setting for Shakespeare's *The Tempest.* In both stories she succeeds in making the reader want to take off immediately for foreign countries.

Elizabeth Cadell is another writer of beguiling little mystery stories with unusual settings. Portugal, England, the Canaries, are her favorite locales. In her books, such as *Come Be My Guest*, she creates unusual people, often drawn with a kind of tongue-in-cheek humor.

Daphne Du Maurier's *Rebecca* is everything that a girl wants in a story of romance. Rebecca, the dead wife of an English Lord, continues to exert her all-pervasive influence over the affairs at Manderley and almost succeeds in wrecking her husband's second marriage. Only toward the end of the book does the reader discover that Rebecca's husband had despised her through their married life. The book is one of passion and mystery, set against the dream setting of a country estate of the English aristocracy. It is fascinating as a piece of writing because the most dominating character in the story is dead. Only by one step at a time does the reader start to gain a picture of her as she really was.

Many young girls enjoy the stories of Edna Ferber. Like the authors already mentioned, Miss Ferber succeeds in creating strong, often aggressive, women living in interesting situations. She appeals to our basically romantic conception of a life filled with exciting problems. *Show Boat, Giant, So Big, The Ice Palace, Cimarron,* succeed in capturing the romantic, almost legendary, overtones surrounding the Mississippi River, Texas, the Illinois prairies, modern Alaska, and the Oklahoma of pioneer days. Each book has at least one character who rises to the level of a folk story hero or heroine.

Robert Nathan's *Portrait of Jennie* is the kind of gentle, beautifully crafted romance that girls find most appealing. It tells of a discouraged New York artist who unexpectedly meets a quaintly old-fashioned little girl at twilight in Central Park. She sings a haunting little song and is delightfully vague about who she is and where she comes from. In subsequent meetings, Jennie matures far faster than the normal time intervals permit. As time goes on Ethan and Jennie's strange relationship grows into love and his failure as an artist turns to success. But the different time dimensions in which they live do not permit the "pat" happy ending that one might expect.

Reading such stories as these, girls may be led eventually to reading some of the great romances such as *Jane Eyre, Wuthering Heights,* or *Green Mansions.* And even if the young reader never grows beyond the books of romance discussed earlier, she knows the satisfactions that come from materials which say that life is more intense and beautiful and mysterious than we suspect.

The historical novel has many of the same characteristics as the romance—an interesting vivid main character; fascinating and sometimes mysterious happenings. But supplementing these elements is a historical setting and often a good deal of fairly accurate factual material about the period. Irving Stone has written a whole series of historical biographies most of which center on some American woman. In *Love Is Eternal* he tells the remarkable story of Mary Todd Lincoln, the Southern belle who visits her sister in the frontier capital of Illinois and falls in love with the gaunt, rugged, young Lincoln. Stone attempts to explain through his story why such a woman should have married the young lawyer and why her later actions, particularly those as first lady, earned her the enmity of subsequent historians. His interpretations may be open to question, but the picture of Mary Todd that he presents is both convincing and intriguing. He has also written of Jesse Frémont in *Immortal Wife* and of Rachel Jackson in *The President's Lady.* Stone's account of Michelangelo in *The Agony and the Ecstasy* and of Van Gogh in *Lust for Life* are also worthwhile reading. For years, *Lust for Life* was the only book even dimly resembling an adequate biography of the tormented artist.

Of course, *Gone with the Wind,* is the most passionately read of the historical novels. One young girl I knew took six weeks to finish the book and at the end she said, "Do you mind if I start all over and read it through again?" This story has the fascination of the ante bellum plantation life of the South. It is filled with descriptions of the white-columned houses, the slaves singing in the warm evening, the scent of blossoms, the beautiful costumes of the women with their hoop skirts and voluminous petticoats, the beruffled but gallant men. Here is that dream life that we should all like to taste but only a very few people experience. Against this backdrop emerges Scarlet O'Hara—beautiful, capable and ruthless—always able to control the turbulent world around her during the social upheaval and changes wrought by the Civil War.

Henry Treece is another writer of history-centered novels. A book typical of his writing is *The Amber Princess* in which he tells of Electra's growing up during the period when her father and uncles go off to the Trojan War to rescue her rather giddy Aunt Helen. She too lives through a period of social upheaval and change. Treece imbues this legendary tale from Greek literature with a flesh and blood reality, adhering at the same time to events.

Much as history and romance have appeal for the maturing reader, the added ingredient of religion may contribute to a book's popularity. Lloyd C. Douglas' book *The Robe* and Thomas Costain's *The Silver Chalice,* both dealing with the crucifixion of Christ and the events it set in motion, have been popular with teenagers. Michener's *The Source,* long as it is, attracts great numbers of readers because it details the stubborn faith of the Jews as they fight overwhelming odds throughout the six-thousand-year history of an ancient town in Israel.

A different kind of historical novel, but still an old favorite is Bess Streeter Aldrich's *A Lantern in Her Hand.* This is a family chronicle, the story of a young couple, who go on a wagon train to Nebraska and build a homestead. Through sickness, drought, loneliness, Abby Deal develops into the strong, matriarchal kind of woman who is capable of holding a large family together.

Girls also like adult stories that center around a woman facing the tribulations of modern life. *Mrs. Mike,* the story of Kathy, a sixteen-year-old Boston girl who is sent to Canada because of a lung difficulty, is a great favorite. Kathy is swept off her feet by a Royal Canadian Mounted Policeman and after marrying him faces a life filled with rugged, primitive conditions. Another favorite is *Winter Wheat,* by Mildred Walker. After spending a year at the University of Minnesota, the young heroine finds it difficult to accept her farming parents and her limited background.

Girls at sixteen or seventeen, then, will like many of the same books that their mothers are reading. But they will not like all of them. They do not like stories that detail the daily routine of a woman on a job or at home, true as this may be to the life they may later lead. They want a story that still holds forth the promise of a life that is splendid and exciting.

Boys at this age choose quite different kinds of literature as they move toward manhood. High on their list are war stories, especially those that describe the thoughts and feelings, the tensions and pressures, experienced by men in the stress of battle. *Von Ryan's Express* is such a story, although it is set not on the battlefield, but in a prisoner of war camp in Italy. Ryan, a newly captured soldier, is the ranking officer in the camp. Although his men despise his rigid discipline, they are kept going because of the sense of order it gives their lives. The book comes to a climax on a POW train taking the imprisoned men to a camp

in Germany. Under Ryan, the men systematically kill
the guards on the train and take it over themselves.
The strong personality of the leading character—a man
almost inhuman in his denial of basic human emotions
—seems the primary reason for the popularity of the
book. The range of popular war stories is wide: *Run
Silent, Run Deep, A Bell for Adano, The Guns of Navarone, The Bridges of Toko-Ri, The Wooden Horse,*
are but a few. These books give the young male a
chance to test himself vicariously. Young men realize
that a Korea or a Viet Nam is always imminent, and it
is quite natural that they need to find out what war
feels like.

Boys, perhaps more than girls, are interested in the
adult novel that presents some aspect of the immediate
social problems of our age. *Black Like Me,* by John
Howard Griffin although not a novel, has all the excitement and tenseness of fiction. The author, a white
journalist, has his skin artificially darkened and experiences the life of the American Negro in the deep South
for a period of six weeks. In his moving account, he
records the constant insults, the strange life of deprivation, the precarious existence of the Negro. But he also
communicates the great sense of human brotherhood
shared by the Negroes among their own. This book has
been widely read and widely discussed by adolescents.
So has *The Ugly American,* by Eugene Burdick and
William J. Lederer. *The Ugly American* is a strong
indictment of America's role in Southeast Asia. It
forcefully points up the ineptness and naiveté of government officials who do not make the effort to understand the rural and village people.

Novels concerned with social injustices, such as
Exodus and *To Kill a Mocking Bird,* are widely read
and discussed by teen-agers. The first book delineates
the confused situation that has evolved among the
British, the Arabs, and the Jews during the founding
of modern Israel. The second exposes the failure of

justice in a small Southern community where a Negro
is unjustly accused of rape.

Stories of contemporary politics, like *Advise and
Consent*, or of the pressures of modern business, such
as *The View from the Fortieth Floor*, have been sought
out and read by the older adolescent who is looking for
information about the nature of modern society, even
though such books offer no solutions.

A related type of book that appeals to boys of this
age is the story set in the near future. This is not a
science fiction tale for the scientific conditions of life
remain much the same as we know them; neither is it
a story of a Utopian society, since the social organization is not idealistically conceived. One of the earliest,
On the Beach, was written by the prolific and imaginative writer, Neville Shute. It is the story of the last
little pocket of human life as deadly radiation advances
towards their remote stronghold. *Fail-Safe* pictures the
situation when the panic button is pushed and computers activate the bombers of the Strategic Air Command for an invasion of Russia. *Seven Days in May* is
similar, suggesting that even in the United States a
group of the military could take over the government
in a well-planned coup. These are terrifying books,
but it should be reassuring that they are popular with
the adolescent, for in spite of his music, his dances, his
clothing styles, his dating habits, he is deeply concerned about the future and what might happen to his
world. He is seeking the solutions to the problems
plaguing society just as mankind has always sought
them.

Boys, as well as girls, are interested in a story domi-
nated by a central character with a vivid, strong personality, either good or evil. *Mutiny on the Bounty*,
the story that Nordhoff and Hall based on the journals
and newspaper accounts of the famous mutiny against
Captain Bligh in the South Pacific, has all the thrill and

excitement of the usual adventure story at sea. But it also has Captain Bligh, a tyrant, an indomitable personality who by sheer will and determination guides a boatload of men over 5,000 miles of ocean to safety after they are set adrift by the mutineers. Equally exciting and commanding as a person is Fletcher Christian, the man who is ultimately prevailed upon by the men to lead the mutiny. In a similar way, Jack Schaefer's *Shane* centers on a pair of rugged individualists. Shane is a drifting gunman who by chance becomes involved in a battle between a Western farmer and the cattlemen who resent the newcomers' fencing in the formerly open range. The two men stand shoulder to shoulder in a final gun fight. Descriptions of personality and value differences give depth to the story, lifting it into the category of a "psychological Western," probably the first of the type

It should be understood, of course, that the popular adult books that young people read will change from generation to generation. A few like *A Lantern in Her Hand, Winter Wheat,* and *Lost Horizon* will continue to be favorites ten years from now, although most of the others discussed in this chapter will become dust laden. Still, the new favorites will have a strong family resemblance to books that the young adult is now reading, because they will be read for the same reason—primarily, for entertainment. And they will continue to represent the basic social thinking of the generation that produces them. In reading such material, the young person is grasping for mature, adult concepts of life. Some may argue that these books present the illusion of maturity rather than maturity itself. But after all, this is the pattern of growth: first must come the big, bold, undifferentiated movements. Then the process of slow and painful refining. So in reading, the child probably needs first to gain the big, bold, often bald outline of the adult world and adult ideas. Then slowly and painfully he will move on to literature that will help him refine and separate the dross from the precious metal.

Bibliography

POPULAR ADULT FICTION

Aldrich, Bess Streeter: *A Lantern in Her Hand.* Appleton, 1928; Tempo. The life of a pioneer family on the Nebraska prairie centers around the mother's courage, vision, and good humor.

Arnow, Harriet: *The Dollmaker.* Macmillan, 1954; Collier. A heroic woman from the Kentucky hills with her family endures the squalor, loneliness, and degradation of a Detroit slum.

Asimov, Isaac: *The Caves of Steel.* Hardback edition out of print; Pyramid. Detective work in a steel-canopied New York City of the future is complicated by prejudice against the robots.

Barrett, William E.: *The Lilies of the Field.* Doubleday, 1962; Popular. A Southern Negro just out of the Army helps four German refugee nuns build a chapel, almost without knowing why himself.

Beach, Edward L.: *Run Silent, Run Deep.* Holt, 1955; Pocket. The skipper of a submarine tells of his action against the Japanese in the Pacific and his problems with his own crew.

Bennett, Jack: *The Hawk Alone.* Little, Brown, 1965; Bantam. A South African hunter faces the problems of old age and modern civilization. Flashbacks to the hunting and war experiences of his youth contrast with his quietly ironic introspection.

————: *Mister Fisherman.* Little, Brown, 1965; Bantam. As a wealthy boy and his Negro fishing guide drift helplessly in the ocean current off Africa, they come face to face with the attitudes that have separated their races.

Borland, Hal: *When the Legends Die.* Lippincott, 1963; Bantam. A Ute Indian boy, "civilized" against his will, be-

comes a hard-riding bronc buster, but later returns to his
people. Set in the early part of this century.

Boulle, Pierre: *The Bridge Over the River Kwai*. Vanguard,
1954; Bantam. A British colonel in a Japanese prison camp
keeps up his men's morale by building a bridge which, in
fact, is an aid to the enemy.

————: *Face of a Hero*. Vanguard, 1956. In a trial story of
suspense and profound characterization, a public prose-
cutor in France knows, but for personal reasons feels that
he cannot reveal, the defendant's innocence.

Bradbury, Ray: *The Illustrated Man*. Doubleday, 1958; Bantam. The fantastic tattoos on a man's torso reveal horrible
and fascinating scenes from the future.

————: *The Martian Chronicles*. Doubleday, 1958; Bantam.
Episodes relating the colonization of Mars in the twenty-
first century combine adventure and social comment.

Breck, Vivian: *Maggie*. Doubleday, 1954. A young San Francisco debutante, married to a dashing gold miner in Mexico, has difficulty adjusting to the harsh life there.

Burdick, Eugene, and Harvey Wheeler: *Fail-Safe*. McGraw,
1962; Dell. A missile-raid warning proves a false alarm,
but by accident one group of bombers is not recalled and
heads on to Moscow.

Cadell, Elizabeth: *Come Be My Guest*. Morrow, 1963. The
guests of the eccentric Baronesa de Narvão are surprised
when she invites them to her lavish entertainment and even
more surprised when she presents them with a staggering
bill!

Caldwell, Taylor: *Dear and Glorious Physician*. Doubleday,
1959; Bantam. This fictional life story of St. Luke concentrates on the conflict in his own mind between faith
in Christ and distrust of a God who permits his creatures
to suffer.

Clark, Walter Van Tilburg: *The Ox-Bow Incident*. Vintage,
1940; Signet. A psychological Western with many different
kinds of characters. A mob in Nevada in 1885 lynches an
innocent man.

Costain, Thomas B.: *The Black Rose*. Doubleday, 1945. This
thirteenth-century romance carries a young English noble-
man to the heart of the Mongol Empire and back again.

————: *Darkness and the Dawn*. Doubleday, 1959. A Roman
slave escapes to fight with Attila the Hun, but eventually
repudiates him because of his barbaric cruelty.

————: *The Last Love*. Doubleday, 1963; Pocket. A French-speaking English girl on the isle of St. Helena in 1815 becomes interpreter and outspoken friend to the exiled Napoleon.

————: *The Silver Chalice.* Doubleday, 1952; Pocket. This re-creation of the New Testament world is based on legends which sprang up after the Crucifixion. It centers around the artisan who fashioned the chalice used to hold the wine at the Last Supper.

Cronin, A. J.: *The Citadel.* Little, Brown, 1937; Bantam. A brilliant young British doctor sacrifices his professional ideals for financial and social success.

————: *The Green Years.* Little, Brown, 1944; Bantam. The story of an orphaned Irish boy and his fierce determination to become a doctor.

————: *The Keys of the Kingdom.* Little, Brown, 1941; Bantam. The life story of a Catholic priest whose missionary efforts among Chinese peasants involve him in man's ageold struggles with the ravages of nature and the darkness of ignorance.

Davies, Valentine: *Miracle on 34th Street.* Harcourt, 1947. The famous story of the myth (and reality!) of Kris Kringle, alias Santa Claus.

Deighton, Len: *The Ipcress File.* Simon and Schuster, 1963; Crest. In a bristling satire of the CIA and Scotland Yard, a British secret agent races across the globe to capture and return a defecting biochemist.

Dodson, Kenneth: *Away All Boats.* Little, Brown, 1954; Bantam. An authentic fictional account of U.S. naval operations in the Pacific in the Second World War, neither exaggerated nor sensationalized.

Douglas, Lloyd C.: *The Big Fisherman.* Houghton, 1948; Pocket. The story of Simon Peter is interwoven with that of an Arabian princess whose life is touched by Christ.

————: *The Robe.* Houghton, 1942; Pocket. The experiences of the Roman tribune who wins Jesus' robe in a dice game lead to his conversion and martyrdom.

Drury, Allen: *Advise and Consent.* Doubleday, 1959; Pocket. In this detailed fictional picture of government processes and people, Congressional intrigue is set in motion when the Senate is called upon to confirm the President's nomination of a new Secretary of State.

Du Maurier, Daphne: *Rebecca.* Doubleday, 1948; Pocket; Wash. Sq. The mysterious atmosphere of an old English estate and the peculiar behavior of the housekeeper arouse

a bride's suspicions concerning her husband's beautiful
first wife.

Erdman, Loula Grace: *The Edge of Time*. Dodd, 1950. Authentic Americana in the story of a woman's journey by
covered wagon from Missouri to the plains of Texas, where
her husband is waiting for her.

Ferber, Edna: *Cimarron*. Doubleday, 1951; Bantam. The pag-
eantry of Oklahoma history is revealed through the stories
of quixotic Yancy Cravat, Sabra the Southern belle he
married, and their family.

———: *Giant*. Doubleday, 1954; Pocket. The grandeur and
harshness of the Texas landscape, the brashness and materialism of Texans, are seen through the eyes of a wealthy
rancher's bride.

———: *Ice Palace*. Doubleday, 1958; Macfadden. Two pio-
neering families in Alaska are followed through three generations. The local color background is pictured in realistic
detail.

———: *Show Boat*. Doubleday, 1951; Pocket. Life on the
"Cotton Blossom floating palace theatre" balances pre-
cariously between idyllic romance and bitter tragedy.

———: *So Big*. Doubleday, 1951; Avon. The story of Selina
DeJong—daughter of a gambler, teacher in a Dutch settle-
ment, wife and widow of a plodding but good-natured
farmer, mother of So Big.

Forbes, Kathryn: *Mama's Bank Account*. Harcourt, 1949; Harvest. Delightful episodes from the life of a family of Nor-
wegian immigrants in San Francisco.

Forester, C. S.: *The African Queen*. Mod. Lib., 1940; Bantam.
To escape from the Nazis a man and woman must take
a broken-down boat down an African jungle river.

———: *Captain Horatio Hornblower*. Little, Brown, 1939;
Bantam. First of the central novels in the Hornblower
series, which now runs to eight books and covers the
career of an English seaman of the Napoleonic era from
midshipman to admiral to his elevation to the peerage.

Fowles, John: *The Collector*. Little, Brown, 1963; Dell. The
horror story of Clegg, a cold-blooded butterfly collector,
and Miranda, a young woman whom he kidnaps.

Freedman, Benedict, and Nancy Freedman: *Mrs. Mike*. Coward, 1947; Bantam. The hardships of life as wife of a
Canadian Mountie in a lonely outpost prove almost too
much for young Katherine Flannigan.

Fuller, Iola: *The Loon Feather*. Harcourt, 1940. The sensitive, introspective story of Oneta, daughter of Tecumseh—her romance with Dr. Reynolds, her respect for her French stepfather, and her loyalty to her own people.

Gallico, Paul: *The Snow Goose*. Knopf, 1941. The quiet, fanciful story of a hunchbacked painter who establishes a bird sanctuary in an abandoned lighthouse along the English coast. It leads up to the stirring climax of the Dunkirk evacuation.

Gann, Ernest K.: *The High and the Mighty*. Sloane, 1953. Strong suspense and absorbing human interest develop when the crew and passengers of an airliner flying from Hawaii to San Francisco face disaster.

Gilbreth, Frank B., Jr., and Ernestine Gilbreth Carey: *Cheaper by the Dozen*. Crowell, 1949; Bantam. A zestful tale of family adventures as Dad prepares his wife and twelve children to carry on without him.

Godden, Rumer: *The River*. Viking, 1959; Compass. The flowing of the river comes to symbolize the cycle of birth, life, and death for a young girl growing up in India.

Goudge, Elizabeth: *The Scent of Water*. Coward, 1963; Crest. In an aura of mysticism and fantasy, an English woman returns to her childhood home where she finds personal fulfillment for the first time in her life.

Griffin, John H.: *Black Like Me*. Houghton, 1961; Signet. The author tells how he blackened his skin and traveled through the Deep South experiencing the terrible predicament of the Negro.

Guareschi, Giovanni: *The Little World of Don Camillo*. Farrar, Straus, 1951; Pocket. The first of a series of delightful books about the never-ending skirmishes between an Italian village priest and his friend-enemy, the Communist mayor.

Guthrie, A. B.:*The Big Sky*. Houghton, 1957; Pocket. The men of the Western mountains, 1830–1843, are representative of the virtues and vices, the rise and the fall, of the American frontiersman.

———: *The Way West*. Houghton, 1949; Pocket. The tensions, folly and courage of a wagon train headed for Oregon in the 1840's are pictured with psychological depth and intensity.

Heinlein, Robert A.: *The Puppet Masters*. Doubleday, 1951; Signet. The mystery of the flying saucers is finally solved in 2007.

Hersey, John: *A Bell for Adano*. Knopf, 1944; Bantam. An Italian-American major's attempts to rehabilitate an Italian town after the Second World War lead to humorous, heart-warming, and frustrating situations. He finds a bell for the town hall, but clashes with military bureaucracy.

————: *The Child Buyer*. Knopf, 1960; Bantam. This harsh satire on American education, misguided patriotism, and materialism, presents a company's efforts to "buy" a poor boy of exceptional intelligence in order to train him to use his ability for the company.

————: *A Single Pebble*. Knopf, 1956; Bantam. A young American engineer, investigating the possibility of building a dam on the Yangtze River, sees the conflict between Chinese traditions and Western technology.

————: *The Wall*. Knopf, 1950; Bantam. The triumph of the human spirit in the face of inevitable defeat is seen in a group of friends who face the Nazi extermination of Jews in a Warsaw ghetto.

Hilton, James: *Lost Horizon*. Morrow, 1933; Pocket; Riverside; Wash. Sq. Conway learns the secret of Shangri-La, a paradise hidden in the Tibetan mountains.

————: *Random Harvest*. Little, Brown, 1943; Pocket. The years 1917–1919 are a blank in the memory of the hero of this romance which takes place just prior to the outbreak of the Second World War.

Hulme, Kathryn: *The Nun's Story*. Little, Brown, 1956; Pocket. A controversial book about a nun who discovers that her interests in surgery and in the underground movement during the Nazi invasion of Holland are more important to her than devotion to religious vows.

Innes, Hammond: *The Wreck of the Mary Deare*. Knopf, 1956. An abandoned ship in the English Channel becomes the center of a stormy sea mystery.

Kaufman, Bel: *Up the Down Staircase*. Prentice, 1964; Avon. A collection of notes, memoranda, and letters presents the frustrating, fascinating first year of teaching in an overcrowded New York City high school where students are underprivileged and teachers are overworked.

Knebel, Fletcher, and Charles W. Bailey II: *Seven Days in May*. Harper, 1962; Bantam. A President of the U.S. in the 1970's sets out to foil a military plot to take over the government.

Le Carré, John: *The Spy Who Came in from the Cold*. Coward, 1964; Dell. British secret agent, Alec Leamas, pretends to defect in order to destroy an East German who has killed the last British agent behind the Iron Curtain.

Lederer, William J., and Eugene Burdick: *The Ugly American.*
Norton, 1958; Crest. Vignettes of inept American diplo-
mats in the fictitious Asian country, Sarkhan, and of a
chicken farmer who succeeds in spite of them.

Lee, Harper: *To Kill a Mockingbird.* Lippincott, 1960; Popular.
A young tomboy sees the quiet life of her small Alabama
town disrupted when her father decides to defend a Negro
accused of rape.

Llewellyn, Richard: *How Green Was My Valley.* Macmillan,
1940; Collier. This saga of a Welsh mining family, told
from the viewpoint of the youngest son, pictures early
labor problems and one family's tensions and tragedies.

MacInnes, Helen: *The Venetian Affair.* Harcourt, 1963; Crest.
An American newspaperman accidentally becomes involved
in a Communist plot to assassinate the French president,
then assists in apprehending the plotters and a master spy.

MacLean, Alistair: *The Guns of Navarone.* Doubleday, 1957;
Wash. Sq. The heroic exploits of a five-man British army
team chosen to knock out the guns which control the ap-
proaches to the eastern Mediterranean islands.

Michener, James A.: *The Bridge at Andau.* Random, 1957;
Bantam. A stirring report of the Hungarian freedom fight-
ers—their revolt, defeat and flight to freedom in Austria.

———: *The Bridges at Toko-ri.* Random, 1953; Bantam. A
short, realistic novel about a resentful, but heroic, jet pilot
in the Korean War.

———: *Hawaii.* Random, 1959; Bantam. Stories of many of
the peoples of Hawaii—Polynesian, American missionary
stock, Japanese, Chinese—are interwoven in a fast-paced
narrative which spans the island's entire history.

Mitchell, Margaret: *Gone with the Wind.* Macmillan, 1939;
Pocket. From this all-time best-seller about Civil War
times, the shrewd Scarlet O'Hara and the dashing Rhett
Butler have become legendary figures, and Tara, the em-
bodiment of the old Southern plantation life.

Nathan, Robert: *Portrait of Jennie.* Knopf, 1940; Popular. A
dreamlike quality pervades this account of a young painter
whose success dates from his first meeting with the strange,
time-defying Jennie.

Nordhoff, Charles, and James Norman Hall: *Mutiny on the
Bounty.* Little, Brown, 1932; Pocket; Riverside. Captain
Bligh's harsh and unjust treatment of his crew on a voyage
to Tahiti brings on mutiny led by first mate, Fletcher
Christian. Suspense holds until the final trial.

O'Connor, Edwin: *The Last Hurrah*. Little, Brown, 1956; Bantam. An old-time Irish politician in a large eastern United States city during his last campaign is seen to be ruthless, corrupt, charming, and intensely loyal.

Sandoz, Mari: *Winter Thunder*. Westminster, 1954. A very short novel about a school bus lost in a Nebraska blizzard and a young teacher's efforts to save the lives of her students.

Schaefer, Jack: *Shane*. Houghton, 1954; Bantam; Riverside. A mysterious, gentle gunman helps the farmers in their fight with the cattlemen and becomes a hero to young Bob Starrett, who tells the story.

Shute, Nevil: *On the Beach*. Morrow, 1957; Apollo; Signet. The only survivors of an atomic war gather in Australia to await their inevitable doom as the poison moves toward them.

Sienkiewicz, Henryk: *Quo Vadis?* Many editions. Against the background of the struggle between paganism and Christianity in the decadent Rome of Nero is set the romance of a beautiful Christian girl and a Roman soldier.

Smith, Betty: *Joy in the Morning*. Harper, 1963; Bantam. The first two years of marriage for a young college couple in the 1920's are threatened by financial insecurity, jealous misunderstandings, and parental disapproval.

————: *A Tree Grows in Brooklyn*. Harper, 1947; Popular. Sensitive Francie Nolan grows from childhood to youth in a slum section of Brooklyn.

Stewart, Mary: *Airs Above the Ground*. Mill, 1965. A romantic thriller for girls set against the background of an Austrian circus featuring the famous white Lippizaner stallions.

————: *Nine Coaches Waiting*. Mill, 1959; Crest. A young governess in an isolated French château fears for her young charge's safety. Their flight provides a fast-moving climax.

————: *This Rough Magic*. Mill, 1964; Crest. A young English actress visiting on the Greek island of Corfu becomes involved in a strange adventure with a retired Shakespearean actor, a friendly dolphin, and a romantic hero.

Stone, Irving: *The Agony and the Ecstasy*. Doubleday, 1958; Signet. This biographical novel about Michelangelo emphasizes the disappointments and triumphs of his art and his personal life.

————: *Love Is Eternal*. Doubleday, 1954. A sympathetic portrait of Mary Todd which opposes itself to the tradi-

tional interpretation of her marriage to Abraham Lincoln.
————: *Lust for Life*. Doubleday, 1954; Pocket. A biographical
novel based on the stormy personal life and career of the
painter Vincent Van Gogh, ending with his suicide at the
age of thirty-seven.
————: *The President's Lady*. Doubleday, 1959. Rachel Jackson's life was saddened and perhaps shortened by an ugly
scandal kept alive by her husband's political enemies.
Stuart, Jesse: *The Thread That Runs So True*. Scribners, 1949;
Scribners. The true-to-life experiences of a schoolmaster
in the Kentucky hills who has to fight for his pupils' respect but wins their affection.
Tolkein, J. R. R.: *The Lord of the Rings*. Houghton, 1954–
1956; Ballantine; Ace. Adult fantasy in this trilogy centers
around the struggles of the inhabitants of Middle Earth
to keep a magic ring from falling into the hands of the
power of darkness. The three separate titles are *The
Fellowship of the Ring* (1954), *The Two Towers* (1955),
and *The Return of the King* (1956).
Treece, Henry: *Amber Princess*. Random, 1963. Richly descriptive retelling of the myth of Electra which carries
the house of Atreus through and beyond the Trojan War.
Uris, Leon: *Battle Cry*. Putnam, 1953; Bantam. Realism, but
not sensationalism, characterizes this account which follows
a Marine battalion from boot-camp training to fighting in
Guadalcanal.
————: *Exodus*. Doubleday, 1958; Bantam. In their struggle
to establish Israel as a modern nation, loyal Zionists face
the hardships of emigration, British opposition, and guer-
rilla warfare with the Arabs.
————: *Mila 18*. Doubleday, 1961; Bantam. A brutally realistic
picture of life in the Warsaw Ghetto during the forty-two
days it held out against the Nazis' attempts to exterminate
the Jews.
Walker, Mildred: *Winter Wheat*. Harcourt, 1944. An introspective story of a Montana girl who blames her parents
when her fiancé breaks their engagement because of the
difference in their backgrounds.
West, Morris L.: *The Ambassador*. Morrow, 1965; Dell. A
controversial novel which resembles certain actual events,
shows the moral crisis of a United States ambassador to
South Vietnam forced by circumstances to support a military coup against the tyrannical but likable president.
Westheimer, David: *Von Ryan's Express*. Doubleday, 1964;

Signet. One thousand prisoners of war in Italy are loaded
into boxcars to be sent to Germany. A sharp American
colonel engineers their escape.

White, Robb: *Torpedo Run.* Doubleday, 1962. A PT boat crew
which has seemed almost invincible chafes under the reg-
ulations of a new, inexperienced skipper.

————: *Up Periscope.* Doubleday, 1956. Ken Braden's first
submarine duty involves a dangerous mission in which
he must find and decipher an enemy code by himself.

White, Theodore H.: *The View from the 40th Floor.* Sloane,
1960; Signet. A publisher struggling to save his two fail-
ing magazines finds himself defending the integrity of the
press against the unscrupulous tactics of powerful stock-
holders.

Wibberly, Leonard: *The Mouse on the Moon.* Morrow, 1962;
Bantam. The tiny Duchy of Grand Fenwick becomes the
first country to land a rocket on the moon. This hilarious
satire is a sequel to *The Mouse That Roared* (Little, 1955).

Wilder, Robert: *Wind from the Carolinas.* Putnam, 1963; Bantam. From the American Revolution to the present the
chronicle of a loyalist family in the Bahamas.

Williams, Eric: *The Wooden Horse.* Abelard, 1958; Berkley.
A rugged story of the escape of two RAF officers from a
German prison camp and their flight to the Baltic.

Wouk, Herman: *The Caine Mutiny.* Doubleday, 1954; Dell.
Willie Keith is the only one who has the courage to defend Lt. Maryk when he is court-martialed for relieving
the insane Captain Queeg of his command.

Chapter 7
The Shocker

Things forbidden have a secret charm.

Tacitus

Most teen-agers cannot resist the inevitable lure of shocking books. Sometimes these books present ideas or values completely different from those to which the young readers have previously been exposed. But more often the teen-agers are interested in the lurid details of the physical aspects of sex and love which they may only have heard whispered about among their friends.

On one hand, as parents we feel it is important for our children to know the whole of life in order to make the right choices on the basis of knowledge, rather than ignorant guesses. On the other hand, we feel that we have a duty to protect our children from the dirty, the vulgar, the seamy side of life, that somehow we must expose them only to ideas we consider ethically and spiritually right.

When we face the problem in a rational way, most of us realize that our children must live in the modern world, bad as it may be. We sense that there is little to be gained by turning one's back on the way life is lived today and attempting to pretend that society is different from what it is. In fact most of us want to be thought of as "modern people" rather than "old-fashioned." And secretly we want our children to be a bit more progressive, a bit more modern, than we ourselves are.

95

But in accepting all the good things of the modern world, we should be less than realistic if we did not acknowledge that some things about life today shock us. Whether we like it or not, our social order surrounds us with a great deal of sexual stimulation. We find it on our billboards, in the ads of respectable magazines, in the marriage and personal problems advice columns of our newspapers, in the barrage of cheap and not so cheap books and magazines on large newsstands, in our motion pictures, in the conversation and stories told at cocktail parties, in the locker rooms of schools. If a child is not to be kept isolated in a dark room at home, we are going to have to accept that he will be exposed to this aspect of our social order as well as to the things we consider desirable. The twentieth century seems more permissive than some societies of the past, but this contention might be difficult to validate. If one reads history and classic literature, he cannot help realizing that man's basic behavior patterns and his interests have not changed through the years. If we start by admitting these things, we must conclude that the solution is not that of isolating children from today's social order. If our child is to be a contemporary among his contemporaries, if he is to be today's child instead of yesterday's, he must be allowed to move through his culture with freedom. What we must attempt is to help him develop a balanced, healthy attitude towards society today. To accomplish this it is recommended that the parent follow certain procedures:

1. When you discover a copy of a lurid book, a girly magazine, or a dirty joke book concealed in your teenager's room, do not act with emotion and embarrassment. He is not some strange monster, nor are his interests unnatural. He is fascinated by this material because he has heard about it from his friends. He has a natural curiosity coupled with maturing and innately healthy desires. So he wants to find out for himself all there is to know about life. Making a scene, destroying the material, accusing your child of shameful desires, may only make him more clever in hiding such reading matter from you. Such reactions on your part may also plant the notion in your child's mind that he somehow is twisted and perverted. However, it is desirable to bring this reading out in the open. So in some subtle way you need to let the child know that you realize he is reading such materials and that you don't intend to attack him for it. When you discover a concealed magazine or book, casually leave it out on a table or on top of the bedspread, but say nothing about it. Try to convey to him the idea that if material is worthy of being read it is not necessary to hide it; that though you yourself do not find such matter interesting, it is a very usual stage in the process of moving toward mature and adult literature.

2. *Keep the channels of communication between you and your teen-age child open.* He needs to discuss his reactions to salacious materials with someone, just as adults find it necessary to pour out particularly shocking bits of information to one another. There is therapy in simply being able to talk about one's feelings. In a study in which individuals were asked to report their memories of reading, many told of being "seared" by the impact of a particular book which presented sex frankly to them for the first time. They were upset, almost nauseated, and yet read on with "fascinated horror." The emotions and reactions were private and very vivid, and the young readers desperately needed to bring them into perspective through the process of sharing them with a sympathetic and perceptive adult. How fortunate if the adolescent is secure enough in his relations with his parents so that he can spill over his reactions to them without fearing he will be condemned or shamed! One way to open channels of communication is through the parents' reminiscences of their own experiences in growing up. The young have

always had a yearning to know what their parents did as children. Therefore the parent may do a great deal to instil confidence in his teen-ager by casually telling of his own reactions to such materials when he was about the same age. Often the child feels free in such a circumstance to pose the questions that are troubling him but which he could not find a way to introduce without seeming blunt.

3. *If your teen-ager can discuss books with you, try to lead him to see how dishonest a picture of human life such salacious materials present.* It is not the subject matter of these books that is bad, but rather the false picture they give of human life. Such stories emphasize the importance of the immediate moment and completely ignore cause-effect relations in which actions have consequences that may change the pattern of life. For example, a youngster who takes part in sports or dramatics or camping is aware that any action at any moment has a reaction: if you miss the pass in a football game, you may lose the down; if you muff your lines in a play the next actor cannot continue as the playwright intended; if you let the campfire rage uncontrolled, your dinner will burn, and so will the forest. Hence stories centering only on immediate moments or elements in life without showing the resulting effects or consequences are basically shallow and untruthful.

4. *Once you realize that your adolescent is seeking answers to the drives that are troubling him, it is important to provide reading materials that are both more valid and literary.* The important thing is that he have a balance in his reading materials instead of reading only this objectionable type. Let's be honest with ourselves. Our own patterns of interest in reading range through a variety of levels, depending upon the mood we are in. Every now and again, even mature readers may pick up a cheap magazine or an erotic book and read it through, being half amused, half in-

volved in it. But the point is that the mature reader
knows exactly what the material is attempting to do
and how to handle his reactions. The teen-ager should
begin to read these magazines and books in the same
way if he is guided towards a balanced reading program.

The above discussion has centered on the subliter-
ary, salacious presentation of sex. But what about the
honest treatment of the same themes in works of
literature such as *Rabbit Run* or *The Catcher in the
Rye* or *The Scarlet Letter* or *Tess of the d'Urbervilles*
or *Romeo and Juliet?* These may also seem overly
frank in presenting the physical side of life. In recent
years, great controversies have raged in one community after another over books recommended or assigned by teachers to their students. Teachers have
been fired; copies of books have been removed from
the library shelves at the request of parents; there have
even been court cases to decide the status of such
reading materials in the educative process. In such
cases the issue is not over the girly magazine or the
sensational potboiler with its vulgarly lurid story.
Libraries and schools do not recommend such materials nor stock them. When these appear in the adolescents' reading fare, it is a private and personal
matter and each parent must handle this for himself.
No, it is rather that the overly zealous adult in many
communities cannot distinguish between real literature and subliterature.

What is it that makes these books different from the
frankly and openly salacious ones—from the "shocker"
that appears every few years and sells widely? The
incidents in the two kinds of books often seem identi-
cal. Why is one defended by librarians, educators, and
teachers as worthy of being read and the other scorned
as worthless?

Answers to these questions involve the whole nature
of literature and its meaning. Professional workers

with literature, even the courts themselves, have recognized the principle that a work of art must be
judged as a whole, not by its individual parts. This
means that a book should not be condemned as "salacious" because of any single incident or group of
incidents or because of certain vulgar words. It must
be looked at as a total entity intended to produce a
given kind of impact on the reader. Often the contention made in defense of a literary work is that it is not
the content per se that makes a book objectionable or
unobjectionable, but rather the manner in which the
content is handled.

What do these arguments mean? A number of years
ago I. A. Richards at Cambridge University pointed
out two very important components of meaning in
literature. On the one hand, he indicated the factor
that might be labeled "plain sense." This is made up
of the incidents, the plot movement, the characters,
and the things they say. The second factor is the
writer's attitude toward these events and characters.
This second quality is sometimes referred to as the
"voice of the writer." The writer consciously or sub-
consciously takes an attitude towards the material he
is presenting and the reader consciously or subcon-
sciously recognizes this attitude. A writer may be
amused by what is happening, he may be shocked by
it, he may be compassionate, he may be approving.

Often the individual who objects to an established
work of literature does so because he is looking only
at certain incidents. *The Catcher in the Rye* illustrates
the problem presented when one reads isolated sections of a book. At the level of "plain sense" the story
is told in the first person by a confused boy who runs
away from a private school and wanders aimlessly
around New York City for forty-eight hours before he
cracks completely and is apparently put into an institution. As part of his surface bravado, Holden Caulfield
swears constantly and uses obectionable four-letter

words. In a hotel he has a prostitute sent to his room when the elevator operator makes the offer. He is constantly thinking about sexual experiences in relation to the girls he meets. He is desperately afraid that men are making sexual advances toward him. These details certainly have a lurid quality, and so a parent may feel that the book could be harmful for his adolescent son or daughter to read. But consider the second component of meaning—what does the author feel about the things that are happening to Holden? In other words what is the voice, the tonality, of the writer? What judgment towards Holden and the society he lives in is the author making? Salinger's attitude is one of great compassion for Holden and his confusion. He implies his own aching desire that life might be better and more meaningful to the boy. His tone is one of profound regret and grief that life must hold such torment and despair for a boy who wants a clean and beautiful world. Thus, the total impact of *The Catcher in the Rye* is something quite different from the individual incidents in the story. The author is not trying to shock the reader by display of sex nor stir up lustful feelings in his young readers. He is honestly trying to picture the agonies a young person faces while growing up.

Another book that has been attacked by some parent groups is *Rabbit Run*. It does have a number of fairly explicit descriptions of the sex act. But the author's purpose is not to expound the glories of sex. Rabbit is a miserable individual: confused, searching, immature. He is still the adolescent basketball player becoming increasingly ludicrous as he ages. The writer's attitude towards Rabbit is one of compassion and sorrow for Rabbit's predicament in the modern world; he does not present Rabbit as admirable, and no reader would come away from his reading of the story with any desire to emulate Rabbit's pattern of life. Thus, it may happen in some very significant literature that certain

events are erotic, even suggestive, but the total effect
of the book is something quite different. This happens
when the writer's attitude towards his materials is
moral and sound.

It is helpful to remind ourselves occasionally of the
basic fact that what a young reader finds in a book is
quite different from what the adult finds. This may be
hard to accept until you introspectively ponder the
patterns of learning. For example, it is a common phe-
nomenon that whenever one learns a new word, he
suddenly finds himself aware of it everywhere. It was
obviously there before, but until a person has consciously learned its meaning, he simply remains un-
aware of its existence. Perhaps you have had the
experience of rereading a book that you read as an
adolescent. It can be a revelation. You may be shocked
to discover all manner of things present in the book
which you never recognized as an adolescent. In an
actual experiment of young people's reactions to certain books considered objectionable by adults, the
youngsters were asked to retell each story in their own
words. The stories they told were quite different from
what was on the pages. Since what we get from a book
depends, in part, on what we bring to it, the incidents that may jolt and repulse the adult reader do
not affect the teen-ager the same way. He does not
have the experience to interpret the actual event, so
he slips by it, and as a result these "objectionable" moments are far less vivid to him. Years ago when *A Tree
Grows in Brooklyn* first appeared, 98 per cent of the
adolescent girls I was teaching read the book. The parents were often shocked by some of the incidents in it,
but without exception the adolescents' reaction was:
"It was so wonderful to see how Francie was able to
grow up into a decent person in spite of her horrible
background." The statement is certainly a somewhat
unsophisticated interpretation of the story, but it does

illustrate the difference in the impact of the book on
the teen-ager from its impact on the adult.

The professional worker who defends the choice of
certain books as "worth reading" maintains that freedom can exist only if people are permitted to examine
not just a prescribed and limited set of ideas, but all
ideas. He believes that freedom demands minds that
have studied and examined the whole spectrum of human life, human ideas, human proposals, and from
this examination and study, made their choices. Basically, the narrow-minded, insecure individual is the
one afraid to examine ideas that run contrary to his set
image of existence. Surely it is not the aim of education to produce this biased, opinionated person with
his intellectual blinders holding him to a limited perspective.

One other attack by well-meaning adults is that art
should be beautiful. Their argument is that there is so
much ugliness, cruelty, and sordidness in the world
that art should be used as an oasis to delight and re-
fresh the mind. In other words, art should be a kind of
"beautiful thought" therapy. But what a pity to deny
an adolescent the opportunity to taste some of the
most aesthetically satisfying works in literature on the
grounds that the subject matter is not "beautiful." In
judging the significance of art, it is not only the pretty,
sweet blending of thought and life that is important,
but rather the ability of the artist to present the profound dilemmas of human beings through an intricately structured form. The great problems of life
involve not only the positive and beautiful side of our
natures, but the dark, evil side as well. From art
should come an absorbing, potent meaning whose impact makes us stop and think, "I see what he is saying."
Whether the critic agrees or disagrees with the interpretation of the artist is not important.

The poets, the philosophers, the religious leaders
throughout the ages, have speculated about the nature

of man. Over and over they have come to the conclusion that man is somewhere in a middle state: part god and angel on the one hand; part animal on the other. With such conflicting drives, man cannot help being a confused creature. So it is quite natural that your son or daughter as he matures is torn between these two opposing forces and is lured at times by the erotic, the lurid, the sensational. Because of a sudden surge of new feelings as he matures, he may turn to books that seem utterly vulgar and distasteful to you. Recognize this as part of his experimentation in finding himself and a direction for his life. Because he is inexperienced, he may make salacious reading choices, just as his choices about the length of his hair, the clothing he buys, the manner of his walk, seem crude and unsuitable. He needs help and guidance, not condemnation. And as he matures, his tastes will refine. Part of the process of refinement will come about through his reading—not the trashy, vulgar pulp materials, but the great works of literature which may show the animalistic nature of man, but which also show that even in the depths of degrading actions man is haunted by a godlike vision of greatness and purity.

Chapter 8
Significant Modern Literature

Old books, as you well know, are the books of the world's youth and new books are fruits of its age.

Oliver Wendell Holmes

A few books published each year are widely acclaimed by critics as worthy of becoming a part of enduring literature. If they continue to be read and praised by sophisticated readers, they join a group of titles that publishers sometimes refer to as "modern classics." While it is difficult to define a modern classic precisely, it is generally more profound than a popular adult novel. Its writing is more skillful: characters are developed with more depth; plot patterns are more intricate in design; and the language used has a subtle flavor not found in ordinary prose. Often the modern classic creates provocative symbols that haunt the imagination. All in all, the significant modern book is something more than just a fascinating story about interesting people.

Ordinarily this is the body of literature to which the adolescent looks after becoming satiated with the popular adult books. Not all young people, however, will develop this taste. In records of student reading kept at the laboratory school at the University of Iowa over several years, about one-third of the books read and admired by able seniors fell in this category, while fifty per cent of their selections remained in the area of popular adult reading.

However, students in the last years of adolescence

prefer contemporary reading and therefore tend to
choose books by significant modern writers. According
to a survey made by the National Council of Teachers
of English among several thousand award-winning students in English, of the forty titles most often mentioned as having the greatest impact, two-thirds were
written during the twentieth century, and more than
half of these, since the Second World War. With few
exceptions, they were books having some critical
acclaim.

Each generation of adolescents selects a group of
titles or authors as "their own." These become the idols
that one must have read and must admire to be "in the
know." In the 1920's, the young adult intellectuals read
Edna St. Vincent Millay and Sinclair Lewis. In the
30's, they were enthusiastic about James T. Farrell,
Thomas Wolfe, and Ernest Hemingway. In the 40's
the preferences were less distinct, perhaps because of
youth's involvement in the Second World War; but
Norman Mailer probably came close to becoming such
an idol, as did Ayn Rand toward the end of the decade.
In the 50's T. S. Eliot, Dylan Thomas, and Albert
Camus were the status authors. The 60's have brought
to the forefront Salinger, Golding, Orwell, Updike,
and Heller.

Though idols change from generation to generation,
they all have certain qualities in common. They are
writers who challenge the conventional assumptions
of the period. They tend to glorify the individual and
his individuality as he struggles against the intolerable
web of contemporary society. They write books that
in idea or situation or language shock the older generation of readers. Each generation's idols express the
adolescent's rebellion against adult society and his
struggle to find some sort of more satisfying direction
or pattern for himself.

Many of these books, although written for the general adult reader, find their major readership among

adolescents after the first wave of popularity. The titles discussed in this chapter are the "mystique" books, that body of literature that today's sensitive young adult reads and cherishes.

One of the books that has had a great impact on several generations of young adults is Somerset Maugham's *Of Human Bondage*. It is the story of Philip Carey between the ages of twelve and thirty. Philip's affliction, a club foot, definitely colors his reactions to the world, but his journey towards maturity is the journey shared by most young intellectuals. He struggles with his religious beliefs, discovers the world of ideas, pursues the dream of an artist's bohemian life, tries to probe and understand the bittersweet torments of love, and finally faces the necessity of making a vocational choice, settling on medicine. At the end of the book, he marries a well-balanced, sweet girl and is ready to take over a country doctor's medical practice. Thus he stumbles into respectability. No other book of the twentieth century seems to have captured so well the storm and torments accompanying the young adult's struggle to find a direction for his life.

J. D. Salinger's *The Catcher in the Rye,* discussed in the last chapter, has been almost phenomenal in its appeal to the teen-age reader. Although it was published in the early 1950's, it did not achieve its wide readership immediately. Holden, the hero, typifies the confused, adolescent male trying desperately to find something clean, pure and beautiful in life. Each tentative attempt is met by pretense, filth, or phoneyness. He is a tangled mass of confusions: confusions about his sexual desires, his vocational aims, his family's treatment, his relationships with his peer group. Holden, more than any character in American literature since Huck Finn, portrays the innermost doubts, fears, the sense of guilt, and the aspirations of the adolescent male.

Another book related in theme to *The Catcher in*

the Rye is John Knowles' *A Separate Peace.* This book also probes the hero's feelings of guilt. The story, told in retrospect, is about the friendship between two boys in a private school. One of the boys, Phineas, has been killed in an accident. His friend the narrator recounts his days at the school, and attempts to assess his own degree of guilt.

Similar in kind but more subtle in its approach to this theme is Albert Camus' *The Stranger.* Camus, a Frenchman, grew up in Algeria and uses this country as the setting for most of his writing. *The Stranger,* told in brittle, clear language, is the story of a young Frenchman who in a moment of sun blindness kills an Arab. He is arrested, convicted, and about to be executed. His strange refusal to make any defense of his actions appeals to the young reader who admires the grand gesture and is fascinated by this depth study of the ultimate meaning of man's life.

Young people also find *A Burnt-Out Case,* by Graham Greene, one of Britain's most prominent novelists, a haunting story. The title refers to a stage in leprosy when the disease has become quiescent and the patient is called "a burnt-out case." The story concerns an architect who wants to renounce any involvement with life. The disease of civilization—striving for wealth and fame—has left him a burnt-out case. He goes to a leper colony in Africa, but life's demands, like the tendrils of a vine, reach out for him. The adolescent identifies with the hero who rejects life.

Still another book significant for adolescents is *The Lord of the Flies,* by William Golding. Here is a story of a group of boys isolated on a tropical island after a plane crash. Immediately they divide into two groups: one seeks to set up an ordered civilization based on justice and right; the other group reverts to primitive savagery. Bit by bit savagery gains control of most of the youngsters and those who supported rationality and morality are on the verge of being overwhelmed. Only the timely arrival of a navy ship prevents the total annihilation of the forces of good. The real impact of the story is at the subjective level, because the reader gains a gradual awareness that Golding is not commenting about the nature of the children, but rather about man and his value systems. He is suggesting that the evil in human life is an active force that must always be met with a united front, else humanity is doomed. And the appalling events in the book are reasonable enough to set the reader wondering, thinking, probing his own thoughts and attitudes.

Carson McCullers' work has had a strong following among adolescents in recent years. Perhaps the most popular has been *The Member of the Wedding* in which Frankie Addams, a twelve-year-old girl, is desperately looking for "the we of me." Frankie's brother is being married this particular summer, and the young girl conceives the strange desire to go with the honeymooners on their wedding trip. She tries to grow up through the trappings of maturity: putting on lipstick; going to the Blue Moon, a tavern; and making a date with a soldier. Through the incidents, the author captures the confusion of the young girl as she moves into adolescence and is faced with new emotions, new situations, and even new status.

For years Ernest Hemingway has appealed to adolescent readers. He is a master at presenting the individual in his struggle to find values in a confusing world. One of his books most widely read by the young person emerging into adulthood is a book written late in Hemingway's life, *The Old Man and the Sea*. It is almost an archetypal study of the battle between man and nature. Santiago, an old broken fisherman, engages in an epic struggle with a huge marlin. After hours of battle, he succeeds in catching the monster only to have his catch devoured by sharks. Yet Santiago's will to fight and subdue the gigantic fish, though in retrospect it may seem irrational and even useless, somehow epitomizes the elusive thing called "spirit" in man. Here is a positive action—this pitting of oneself against nature's forces—that has meaning for a man.

The present generation of adolescent readers has had high regard for John Steinbeck. Surprisingly, it is not *The Grapes of Wrath,* perhaps the book best known to adult generations, that they are reading as much as his shorter books—*Cannery Row, Tortilla Flat,* and *Of Mice and Men.* In some recent papers written by adolescents on Steinbeck, one student commented that he thought Steinbeck's people were adults running away from society and its demands. He saw them as people escaping social pressures and doing it with a clear conscience. Another student expressed the opinion that Steinbeck frequently pictured people imprisoned by society, by their own moral code, or by their physical bodies. To him Steinbeck's characters escaped by accepting themselves and whatever life had doled out. Thus it would seem that what young people find in Steinbeck is not so much social protest as the struggle of the human spirit to break free from society's restrictions.

A man who has been let down by society is the tragic hero of Arthur Miller's popular play *Death of a Salesman.* Willy Loman, a salesman, has spent his life on the road, accepting and enjoying a world of part-time associations and partial responsibilities. Gradually, as Willy stumbles toward awareness, the reader too realizes that Willy has lived his life according to false values.

Very different are the Utopian books. Two of the most popular with teenagers are *Brave New World* and *1984.* In *Brave New World,* Aldous Huxley wanted to show what might ultimately happen to a society that carried psychological conditioning to the extreme. In the world he creates, no one can be unhappy because he is conditioned for his ultimate place

in life from the prenatal stage on. In *1984*, George
Orwell, a lifelong opponent of totalitarianism, sketches
a society based on complete thought control of each
individual citizen. The purpose of both of these Utopian books is to point out the dangerous trends present
in society today. These books are far more widely read
than are such books as Edward Bellamy's *Looking
Backward* which presents a visionary picture of the
perfect society.

Another author of social protest appreciated by adolescents today is Sinclair Lewis, even though his books
were written thirty to forty years ago. Young people
enjoy reading *Main Street* and *Babbitt* because they see
in Lewis' picture of the sham and pretense of middle
class Midwestern life in the 20's the same sham and
pretense present today. They respond to his clever
parodies of advertising slogans and small-town newspaper writing, to the habits, speech, and thoughts of
such characters as Babbitt. Yet their primary love is
Arrowsmith in which Lewis not only satirizes many of
the aspects of society, but shows the struggle of a
young medical student seeking a direction for his life
and his work.

At first glance, Harper Lee's *To Kill a Mockingbird*
would not appear to attract the adolescent reader,
since it is told from the point of view of a very young
child. This story of racial injustice has a powerful message for young people who are appalled by the effects
of prejudice.

One of the most articulate and impassioned writers
on the race issue is James Baldwin. Baldwin suggests a
reversal of white and Negro roles with startling implications. In earlier racial literature, he contends, the
writers implied that the Negro was trying to break out
of his cage into the white man's world. Baldwin suggests that it is the white man who is in a cage, even
though it is one of his own making, and he cannot
break out of it into the Negro world and psyche. He

therefore sees the white man afflicted with the self-induced disease of discrimination.

Each generation of sensitive adolescents favors some writers their parents do not approve of or understand. Because they feel that no people before them ever faced the same problems, the same feelings, the same world that they face, they look for the authors who help them express this uniqueness. It is his own world for which the adolescent reader searches, even though in most of its underlying aspects it is the same world that man has always struggled to understand. And the significant writer for adolescents is the one who reacts to the factors in this unique world and makes a meaningful synthesis of them.

Bibliography

Agee, James: *A Death in the Family*. Obolensky, 1957; Avon. The disruption of a family circle by the death of the father.

Baldwin, James: *Go, Tell It on the Mountain*. Dial, 1963; Universal Library, Dell. A frank picturing of the attempts of Negro migrants to Harlem to find meaning through religion.

————: *The Fire Next Time*. Dial, 1963; Dell. Articulate and impassioned nonfiction, dealing with the plight of the Negro and society's responsibilities.

Buck, Pearl: *The Good Earth*. Day, 1931; Pocket; Wash. Sq. Through persistent labor and a bit of luck, a Chinese peasant rises slowly to become a wealthy landowner.

Camus, Albert: *The Stranger*. Knopf, 1948; Vintage. An existential exploration of life as a man awaits execution in Algeria.

————: *The Plague*. Knopf, 1948; MLCE. The actual outbreak of bubonic plague in a city is symbolic of the plague of modern life in modern society.

Cather, Willa: *My Ántonia*. Knopf, 1918; Sentry. The experiences of a Bohemian girl on the Nebraska prairies as she grows to middle age.

————: *Death Comes for the Archbishop*. Knopf, 1927. Two priests work to re-establish the Catholic faith in the huge area of New Mexico during the nineteenth century.

Eliot, T. S.: *The Cocktail Party*. Harcourt, 1949; Harvest. A poetic drama of lives changed and problems faced through the influence of an unusual guest.

Faulkner, William: *Light in August*. Random, 1932; MLCE. Three strangely intertwined stories dealing with three different kinds of outcasts. Perhaps the most easily grasped of the difficult but rewarding works of this novelist.

Fitzgerald, F. Scott: *The Great Gatsby*. Scribners, 1925; Scribners. The classic picture of aimless, wealthy society in America during the 1920's.

————: *Tender Is the Night*. Scribners, 1934; Scribners. A psychiatrist marries his wealthy patient and, in the end is the person most in need of help.

Forster, E. M.: *Passage to India*. Harcourt, 1924; Harvest. Misunderstandings and tensions between the British and the Indians suggest universal tensions between peoples.

Golding, William: *Lord of the Flies*. Putnam, 1959; Capricorn. A group of boys stranded on an island Eden reverts to primitive savagery and ritual.

Greene, Graham: *A Burnt-Out Case*. Viking, 1961; Bantam. A successful architect sentences himself to life among Congolese lepers.

————: *The Power and the Glory*. Viking, 1946; Compass. A drunken priest battles Mexican politics and dies in a way he could not live.

Heller, Joseph: *Catch 22*. Simon and Schuster, 1961; Dell. A frank presentation of the lives and frustrations of men in the airforce as they pile up enough missions before being rotated home.

Hemingway, Ernest: *A Farewell to Arms*. Scribners, 1929; Scribners. A young couple escapes the rigors of the First World War only to undergo a deeply personal tragedy.

————: *For Whom the Bell Tolls*. Scribners, 1940; Scribners. Love, lost causes, and unselfishness against the background of the Spanish Civil War.

————: *The Old Man and the Sea*. Scribners, 1952; Scribners. An old man and a young boy seek out the sources of faith and respect in a small boat off the Cuban coast.

————: *The Sun Also Rises*. Scribners, 1926; Scribners. A

number of expatriates after the First World War live and travel through Europe, each in his way a cripple.

Hersey, John: *Hiroshima.* Knopf, 1946; Bantam. The author's visit to Hiroshima results in an account of the effect of the atomic blast on the lives of six survivors.

————: *A Single Pebble.* Knopf, 1956; Bantam. The author captures the great strength and dignity of an illiterate man who pulls boats up the rapids of the Yangtze River.

Hesse, Hermann: *Demian.* Harper, 1965; Bantam. The story of Emil Sinclair's youth dramatizes the dilemma of the marked man, the quasi-criminal hero.

Huxley, Aldous: *Brave New World.* Harper, 1932; Bantam. A satirical view of a future society built on psychological conditioning of human beings.

Joyce, James: *A Portrait of the Artist as a Young Man.* Harper, 1932; Compass. The childhood and early manhood of Stephen Dedalus, who is seeking wings with which to escape his birthright.

Kafka, Franz: *The Metamorphosis.* Vanguard, 1946. A young man awakens to find himself transformed into a giant insect.

————: *The Trial.* Knopf, 1957. Human dignity is the subject of this unfinished novel about a man's attempt to seek justice from a faceless authority.

Knowles, John: *A Separate Peace.* Macmillan, 1960; Bantam. A young man revisits the prep school where, as a student, he was involved in the death of his best friend.

Koestler, Arthur: *Darkness at Noon.* Macmillan, 1941; Bantam. An idealistic revolutionary grapples with his principles when ordered by superiors to make a false confession.

Lee, Harper: *To Kill a Mockingbird.* Lippincott, 1960; Popular. Prejudice, courage, and misunderstanding are shown against the background of a small Southern town.

Lewis, Sinclair: *Arrowsmith.* Harcourt, 1925; Signet. A young doctor is torn between his desire to devote his life to research and the pressures to become a wealthy, self-satisfied practitioner.

————: *Babbitt.* Harcourt, 1922; Signet. A midwestern businessman and the conventions of his life are so typical that his name has become the word in the English language used to describe such a person.

————: *Main Street.* Harcourt, 1920; Signet. A minute and satirical view of boredom in a small Minnesota town.

McCullers, Carson: *The Heart Is a Lonely Hunter.* Houghton,

1940; Bantam. A group of strangely different, lonely people in a Southern town communicate their troubles to a deaf-mute.

————: *The Member of the Wedding.* Houghton, 1946; Bantam. A twelve-year-old girl has difficulty understanding why she cannot accompany her brother on his honeymoon.

Maugham, W. Somerset: *Of Human Bondage.* Doubleday, 1915; Pocket; Vintage. The childhood and young manhood of Philip Carey, who battles with himself and with society to find his place in it.

Miller, Arthur: *Death of a Salesman.* Viking, 1949; Compass. A drama of Willie Loman, an aging salesman who finds the clichés he has lived by are false.

O'Neill, Eugene[1]: *Ah, Wilderness!* 1932. The drama of the confusion of an adolescent boy facing the mature world.

————: *Beyond the Horizon.* 1920. In this early O'Neill play, two brothers' love for the same girl forces each into a life pattern he despises.

————: *The Hairy Ape.* 1922. A bitter and ironic play of a ship stoker's attempts to prove himself better than an animal and, defeated, being crushed by an ape in the zoo.

Orwell, George: *Animal Farm.* Harcourt, 1954; Signet. Farmer Brown's animals revolt and set up a socialistic state ruled over by the pigs.

————: *1984.* Harcourt, 1949; Harcourt; Signet. Two young people rebel against a futuristic society which places no value on truth, love, and history.

Pasternak, Boris: *Dr. Zhivago.* Pantheon, 1958; Signet. The poetic spirit of a young man brings him into conflict with officialdom during the Russian Revolution in this long and difficult novel.

Paton, Alan: *Cry, the Beloved Country.* Scribners, 1948; Crest. An African minister seeks the sources of evil which caused the downfall of members of his family.

Remarque, Erich Maria: *All Quiet on the Western Front.* Little, Brown, 1929; Crest. Classic novel of war's horror and its uselessness.

[1] A three-volume collection of the O'Neill plays is published by Random House. Several individual plays and groupings of plays are available in several paperback editions. *Ah, Wilderness!* and *Beyond the Horizon* are available in *Ah, Wilderness! and Other Plays,* published by Modern Library. *The Hairy Ape* may be found in *Emperor Jones, Anna Christie, and The Hairy Ape,* also published by Modern Library.

Saint-Exupéry, Antoine de: *Night Flight*. Century, 1932; Signet. Terrible sense of personal responsibility of pilots and officials in early days of an airmail service in South America.

————: *Wind, Sand and Stars*. Reynal, 1939; text ed., Harcourt. Excitement, philosophy, and a sense of wonder in the early days of flying.

Richter, Conrad: *The Light in the Forest*. Knopf, 1953; Bantam. A white boy raised by Indians suffers from mixed loyalties on the New York frontier.

Salinger, J. D.: *The Catcher in the Rye*. Little, Brown, 1951; Bantam. Two days in the life of a prep school runaway who feels compassion for youth and distaste for the sham of adult society.

————: *Franny and Zooey*. Little, 1961; Bantam. A short novel about members of the Glass family in which childhood struggle is contrasted with adult despair.

Sartre, Jean-Paul: *No Exit*. Knopf, 1947; Vintage. A symbolic play in which the characters discover that society can be its own worst enemy.

Shaw, George Bernard: *Pygmalion*. 1916; Penguin. In this lighthearted play, Henry Higgins, an English linguist, undertakes to pass off a flower girl as a duchess by re-forming her speech.

Steinbeck, John: *The Grapes of Wrath*. Viking, 1939; Bantam; Compass. The Joad family survives despite death, harassment, and apparent defeat in their efforts to escape the Oklahoma dust bowl in the thirties.

————: *Of Mice and Men*. Viking, 1937; Bantam; Compass. The tragic friendship of a migrant worker and a giant halfwit whose dreams are thwarted by misunderstanding and death.

————: *The Pearl*. Viking, 1947; Bantam. An Indian family finds a monstrous pearl and discovers that good fortune does not always bring happiness.

————: *Tortilla Flat*. Viking, 1935; Bantam; Compass. The carefree, simple life of six men is contrasted with the complexities of society.

Undset, Sigrid: *Kristin Lavransdatter*. Knopf, 1935. A trilogy tracing life and romance in 14th century Norway.

Updike, John: *Rabbit, Run*. Knopf, 1960; Crest. A frank treatment of the failure of a former high school athlete to cope with his changed status in the adult world.

Warren, Robert Penn: *All the King's Men*. Harcourt, 1953;

Mod. Lib.; 'Bantam.' The rise to power and ultimate downfall of a demagogue are strikingly depicted in this novel
based on the notorious career of Huey Long.

Wilder, Thornton: *The Bridge of San Luis Rey.* Harper, 1927;
Wash. Sq. A Franciscan friar inquires into the lives of
five people killed in the collapse of an ancient Inca bridge
in colonial South America in order to discover if it was
an accident or divine plan.

Williams, Tennessee: *The Glass Menagerie.* Random, 1945;
New Directions. A drama presenting Tom Wingfield's
memories of his mother and sister imprisoned by their
artificial sense of gentility.

Wolfe, Thomas: *Look Homeward, Angel.* Scribners, 1929;
Scribners. The childhood and adolescence of Eugene
Gant form the center of this long semi-autobiographical
novel set in a decadent Southern town.

————: *You Can't Go Home Again.* Harper, 1940; Dell.
George Webber, a successful writer, experiences failure
in his attempt to see his home town through the eye of
innocence.

Woolf, Virginia: *To the Lighthouse.* Harcourt, 1927; Harvest.
Art, death, and the meaning of human and mystical relationships are explored in the setting of a seaside guest
house.

Chapter 9
The Place of the Classics

A classic is something that everybody wants to have read and nobody wants to read.

Mark Twain

Making a richer life for our children is part of the great American Dream. The immigrant coming to America was willing to undergo great personal deprivation because of his hope that his children would have a better life. The pioneer moving westward was enticed by a similar dream. Even today parents want their children to have all the advantages they feel they themselves have missed.

Among such advantages is an understanding of music, art, literature, the drama. Often parents develop a kind of anxiety about these cultural experiences. They complain when the adolescent brings home car stories or girls' romances or science fiction. They feel he should be selecting *Silas Marner, King Lear,* or *David Copperfield* because they are the respected classics.

Just what is a classic? A cliché often used is that it is a work "that has stood the test of time." It has managed to survive while the majority of its contemporaries have been forgotten. Like many clichés, this one is partly true. A classic is a book written some time ago. There is no arbitrary time line, but most books now considered classics were written before the twentieth century.

Obviously, to survive a book must have certain en-

during qualities. Great literature must confront the
reader with one of the eternal dilemmas of human life.
It may show the pettiness and absurdities of human
beings, point out the transfiguring beauty of love,
make the reader aware of the ironies in human existence, show how the human spirit transcends the
immediate bounds of suffering, depict the feelings of
alienation and loneliness of the individual. Great literature may provide a vision of a possible better world
that men might achieve except for their own natures,
or perhaps present the conflict between the laws of
the social order and the natural law the individual
feels within himself. Literature, as long as it has existed, has expressed these yearnings of the human
spirit, as it struggles to find value in experiences. Inevitably the book that becomes a classic of literature
has as its theme a profound, mature, and significant
appraisal of human life.

The classic is enriched by timeless symbols. The
story itself, its images, its details, transcend the immediate age in which they were conceived and can be
understood by generation after generation of readers.
The stories of Mary and Martha, of the prodigal son,
of the good Samaritan in the Bible carry the same
basic understandings across cultural boundaries and
across two thousand years of time. And for each generation, for each man, the story may have a specific
meaning. For different readers, Captain Ahab's pursuit of the great white whale, Moby Dick, might represent man's search for God, labor's fight against capital,
man's pursuit of woman, the fight of science against the
humanities, the struggle of society against individual
freedom. The writer's symbolism expresses the deepest,
most unresolved problem troubling the reader.

But a classic has more than ageless symbolism. It
has also a magnificence of structure that cannot be
catalogued and dissected and yet produces an elusive,
deep satisfaction. The choice of words, the ordering of

details, the use of symbols, seem exactly right for the theme the writer is developing. A reader may return to a classic, and each time he will take pleasure in its language and meaning.

There is no doubt that the classics of literature represent man's finest use of language. No wonder we want our children to know them. But it is also true that classic literature is the most difficult, the most subtle, and the most mature expression of human beings. Therefore, it is no surprise that an understanding and enjoyment of the classics comes, if at all, fairly late in the reader's growth.

Recently a class of seventy-five college seniors and graduate students were asked when they began reading the classics on their own. One or two indicated that they read some Dickens with real enthusiasm in late childhood and in junior high school. A few said that they "sort of" enjoyed dramatizing *A Midsummer Night's Dream* in ninth grade. A few more mentioned becoming interested in certain Victorian novels in the last years of high school. But the majority indicated that they were sophomores or juniors in college before they came to a real and inspired "liking" for the classics of literature. When pressed to state an honest preference between contemporary or classic reading matter, most admitted that they still preferred Tennessee Williams to Shakespeare and enjoyed Salinger more than Thomas Hardy.

Still parents persist in feeling that even though the adolescent doesn't like or understand a classic it in some way is still "good for him" and that he "will someday be glad he was forced to read it." The records of thousands of readers indicate that this is not true. One usually comes to thoroughly dislike what he is forced to read and cannot understand. One grows slowly toward an enjoyment of the classics through the reading patterns sketched in earlier chapters of this book. The following are some of the classics that have appeal for numbers of adolescents at various steps in their reading maturation.

FROM THE ANCIENT WORLD

The single most important book in Western culture is undoubtedly the Bible. In the early days it was the only book available and readers immersed themselves in its pages, reading and rereading the old, familiar stories. It might almost be called a complete library, for within its covers it contains adventure stories, stories of daily life, romance, history, law, philosophy, and poetry. Because the Bible was an integral part of people's lives, its rhythms of language have influenced the style of great writers and speakers for centuries. Thus any ultimate understanding of Western art forms and Western culture requires some familiarity with the Bible. Many adolescents decide at some point to read the entire Bible. Usually they set themselves a quota of reading for each day, but like most self-improvement programs, this one bogs down in good intentions before too many days pass. Therefore it might be helpful to suggest to your child a "selected" reading program from the Bible, perhaps Genesis, Exodus, Ruth, Samuel, and one of the four Gospels. This will give the young person a body of basic stories that have been echoed throughout the writings and thinking of the entire Western World.

Recently rediscovered by teen-age readers is ancient Greek tragedy. For years this material was available only in literal and labored translations that were both difficult and obscure. But in the last twenty years there have been a number of new modern translations. In these translations the similarity between the Greeks' problems and ours today are strikingly revealed. And because of the stark simplicity of the plots, adolescents find these plays easy to comprehend. One of the better collections is *Ten Greek Plays,* a paperback anthol-

ogy of representative plays from Aeschylus, Sophocles
and Euripides, and one play from Aristophanes. Probably most adolescents discover Greek tragedy when
they read *Oedipus Rex* or *Antigone,* the two great
plays of Sophocles, or the *Medea* of Euripides.

The long epic poems of Homer, the *Iliad* and the
Odyssey, are fine adventure reading for adolescents if
good contemporary translations are used. The *Iliad*
recounts the events of the Trojan War caused when
Paris of Troy eloped with Helen, the wife of the
Greek, Menelaus. The *Odyssey* is the poetic account
of Ulysses' adventures during his long, wandering
return from that war. Like the Bible, the two epics are
almost fundamental background reading for anyone
who wants to understand Western literature. Homer's
two stories have had a resonating impact on the writers
of the world, and references to the tales frequently
appear in contemporary works.

In addition to the individual works from the ancient
world, some young people are fascinated by the stories
of Greek mythology. Such an interest ordinarily develops in late elementary school days or early in the
junior high school period, but it may come as late as
the college level when the young person becomes
seriously interested in the study of literature. There
are numbers of volumes dealing with the Greek myths.
Probably one of the most authoritative is Edith Hamilton's *Greek Mythology.* An interest in myth is worth
encouraging, for the ancient myths are the prototypes
of modern allusions.

FROM ENGLISH LITERATURE

English literature provides a wealth of classics for
the young reader. Frequently, the sensitive and intelligent boy will become enthralled by the tales of King
Arthur and his Round Table. Such a youngster will
probably find his most satisfying account in a modern-

ized version of Malory's *Morte d'Arthur*. A relatively
small number of teen-agers will find Shakespeare rewarding. The plays that are most nearly comprehensible to adolescents are *Romeo and Juliet*, a story of
adolescent love and marriage; *The Taming of the
Shrew*, the madcap, slapstick comedy of a man who
tames a shrewish wife with too much kindness; and
The Merchant of Venice, a drama of life's injustices
and men's trickery. A few sensitive girls find *A Midsummer Night's Dream* delightful. But in general, the
great tragedies are beyond the comprehension of most
high school students; and the great comedies require
so much explanation that they cease to be amusing. Of
course, many English teachers do make Shakespeare
exciting for young people in the classroom.

Robinson Crusoe, the marvelous adventure tale written by Daniel Defoe, is a boy's book. Defoe intended
his novel to demonstrate that a civilized man cast into
a primitive society could solve his problems through
reason. But the average reader enjoys the story for the
details of Crusoe's survival: the way he builds a hut,
finds food and clothing, protects himself from attack.

The next three nineteenth-century books are similar
in their appeal; the young person who likes one of
them will usually read the other two with equal enthusiasm. They are *Jane Eyre, Wuthering Heights*, and
Green Mansions. *Jane Eyre* and *Wuthering Heights*
were written by sisters, the daughters of a remote
country minister. But they poured into the books all
of their mystical, romantic longings for a life burning
with intensity. Their story of love is a perennially
haunting one. The heroes of the stories, Mr. Rochester
and Heathcliff, often become the dream model of the
kind of man that the reader would like to marry. *Green
Mansions*, written by a botanist, shares some of the
basic qualities of appeal of the other two, but the
story is very different. Set in the jungles of South
America, it is the story of a man captured by a primi-

tive tribe of Indians, and his discovery of a mysterious woman who inhabits a sacred grove.

Charles Dickens still holds charms for the maturing reader. Teen-agers are impressed by Sidney Carton's self-sacrifice in the romance of the French Revolution, *A Tale of Two Cities*. Others find *David Copperfield* most appealing for its picture of the hero's journey from childhood into manhood. But perhaps the most popular of Dickens' novels for the adolescent is *Great Expectations*. Pip, an orphan boy, is suddenly befriended by a mysterious benefactor and is taken from his lowly life with Joe and Biddy to become a young gentleman living in London. He gradually finds himself too refined for his old friends and his old, familiar ways of life. Not only is Dickens concerned with universal human emotions and situations, but he fills his novels with galleries of colorful characters and fascinating events.

Many young adults become absorbed in the works of Thomas Hardy, pessimistic as they are. The two favorites of adolescent readers are usually *Tess of the d'Urbervilles* and *The Mayor of Casterbridge*. Tess is a simple country girl, a descendant of a once proud and aristocratic family. She is seduced and bears an illegitimate child. Later when she falls in love and marries, her husband deserts her when she reveals her past. Here is all the unfairness of the world which the adolescent senses and now sees presented in great art. *The Mayor of Casterbridge* tells of the fall of a highly successful businessman, who, while drunk, had sold his wife to a stranger. Slowly the web of circumstances tightens around him until his whole house of cards tumbles. Hardy, perhaps more than any other writer within the last hundred years, comes close to approximating the Greeks in their construction of tragedy.

Because Robert Louis Stevenson is so much a children's favorite, we forget that he is truly a classic writer. Because he chose as the subject for his novels high adventure, mysterious characters, plots and counterplots, his superb artistry is often overlooked. *Treasure Island* is a beautifully crafted work, and some of his other books, among them *Kidnapped, The Master of Ballantrae,* or *Dr. Jekyll and Mr. Hyde* are real masterpieces. In Stevenson's novels as in Dickens', the excitement of the story often carries the young reader through the complex sentences and elaborate vocabulary.

Joseph Conrad stands at the line of demarcation between the Victorian and modern styles of writing. Like the Victorians, he tells a complex story involving strange and complex characters. Like the moderns, his stories probe deeply into psychological problems. Most widely read of Conrad's novels by the young adult is *Lord Jim,* the story of a young seaman who chooses in an emergency to save his own life rather than the lives of his passengers. Jim has a deep inner need to find some way of expiating his sense of guilt—to find some way that he can live with himself. The story takes place in the Indian Ocean and the tropical jungles of the southern part of Asia. Thus it is intriguing not only because of the moral problem involved, but also for the romantic setting.

FROM AMERICAN LITERATURE

From American literature, adolescent boys often discover the tales of James Fenimore Cooper. While Cooper's stories resemble museum pieces because of their quaint, old-fashioned qualities, they still have an undeniable charm. In the nineteenth century, they reflected what Europeans believed was true about the American Indian, and to this day they color Europeans' judgment of America. *The Last of the Mohicans* and *Deerslayer* are filled with the tense struggle of the new settler against the wilderness and against the red man who inhabited it. They still excite the imagination of the young reader who can lose himself in these tales of adventure.

Nathaniel Hawthorne's *The Scarlet Letter* is a great favorite with the more mature adolescent reader. In one study of adolescent reading interests, it was the only noncontemporary work included among the top twenty favorites of a group of bright eleventh- and twelfth-grade students. *The Scarlet Letter* has the dark somber quality of Puritanism. But its portrayal of people who transgress the code of their society and who live with a sense of personal guilt is both absorbing and provocative for today's adolescent.

Herman Melville, one of the two or three most important American novelists, does not find a wide readership among young people. *Moby Dick* is sometimes enjoyed in simplified and cut versions which make it just an adventure or sea story, but in such a version it loses the very qualities that make it the great work it is. Perhaps most popular with teen-agers is *Billy Budd*, Melville's last work. Through extremely difficult and complex prose it tells of a handsome, morally upright, young sailor who is impressed into British navy service and comes face to face with evil in the person of one of his superior officers. He is ultimately destroyed by this officer. This situation—one of man-created injustice—confounds a young reader, yet *Billy Budd*, like similar stories, is a great favorite.

Of the great American writers, Mark Twain is by all odds the favorite of the adolescent reader. From the good-hearted humor of *Tom Sawyer* or the more serious story of *The Prince and the Pauper*, he may move on to the fun of *Life on the Mississippi*, *Innocents Abroad*, or *Roughing It*. Later he may enjoy *A Connecticut Yankee in King Arthur's Court*. This book usually appears to teen-agers as a simple frolic through the Middle Ages, and they miss the vitriolic attacks that Twain makes on the Church. Some may delight in *Puddin' Head Wilson*, an elaboration on the theme of

The Prince and the Pauper. But sooner or later they will read the unique American masterpiece *The Adventures of Huckleberry Finn.* *Huckleberry Finn* is not a sequel to *Tom Sawyer* as many assume. It is a seriously crafted novel dealing with a multitude of themes all beautifully expressed through the visions of Huck as he floats down the Mississippi River. The tale of Huck Finn can be enjoyed by the youngster simply as a good story. Then it is best to put it aside for several years. For in this book Twain has presented two different visions of the world, neither of which the reader can see at that in-between stage when he is neither child nor adult.

Although Stephen Crane's *Red Badge of Courage* is short, it is perhaps the most intense study of a young boy's conception of war and his actual reaction under fire. Its emotional impact reaches the sensitive adolescent reader, but for many the story is so deceptively simple that it leaves them completely unmoved.

A perennial favorite with junior high school students is Edgar Allan Poe. Young people glory in the bizarre, the scary, the mysterious. This is the age when they thoroughly enjoy a good horror movie or delight in an eerie television program. No writer has ever produced these feelings more skillfully than Poe. It seems only logical to utilize this innate interest of the junior high school youngster, and introduce him to the master writer of some of the greatest horror stories ever created.

FROM WORLD LITERATURE

European classics are available through translation. Everyone talks about and everyone recommends *Don Quixote,* that strangely moving Spanish work whose central character is a man who prefers to live in the age of knighthood instead of his own time. The hero valiantly tries to interpret everything that happens to him within the context of his imagined world. A complete translation runs to almost a thousand pages. Most readers find it more palatable to read a shortened or retold version and come to know this gallant, impractical Don in this way.

Two great favorites of fifteen- and sixteen-year-old readers are Alexandre Dumas' *The Count of Monte Cristo* and *The Three Musketeers*. These stories of intrigue at a high level of sophistication offer exciting fare to the young reader. Another French novel often read by sensitive adolescents is Victor Hugo's *Les Misérables*. It is a long, long story depicting the miseries of the lower classes in France. Since the young adult is looking for some code of values in his reading, this exposure of social injustice affects him deeply. But the French work to which adolescents most often lose their hearts is Rostand's *Cyrano de Bergerac*. Here is Cyrano, a great spirit imprisoned in the body of a clown. Here the reader can visualize renunciation, fidelity, romance, the grand gesture—everything that helps to make man just a little lower than the angels.

Of the great Russian novels, *Crime and Punishment*, by Dostoevsky, is probably the one most frequently read by the adolescent. It begins as a young student carries out his strange whim of murdering an old and repulsive pawnbroker. The novel shows him in the days immediately following the crime as he wrestles with his guilt.

What then is the pattern of reading to expect from the adolescent in respect to the classics? A few classics such as *Treasure Island, Tom Sawyer, The Prince and the Pauper, Alice in Wonderland,* may be read at a relatively young age. In junior high some young people will want to read the *Iliad* and the *Odyssey*. They may also find *Robinson Crusoe* much to their liking. At fifteen or so they will be at the point where *The Count of Monte Cristo* and *The Three Musketeers* will be exciting. Ordinarily this is the age when *Romeo and*

Juliet may be most meaningful to the romantically in-clined girl. At sixteen or seventeen, the adolescent girl may enjoy *Jane Eyre* and *Wuthering Heights,* and some boys will appreciate *The Red Badge of Courage* or Shakespeare's *Julius Caesar.*

Parents should realize that an interest in the classics develops slowly. The interest patterns that control your youngster's choices in his usual personal reading will determine what he reads among those books lab-eled "classics." Great literature is written by mature artists about mature concerns, and it therefore follows that only a few of these books center on the subjects most dear to the adolescent's heart: adventure, mys-tery, teen-age problems, romance.

Because the classics are the pinnacle of man's liter-ary achievement, it is quite natural to want our chil-dren to appreciate and value the views of life they present. In our eagerness to share the best of the adult world with them, we shove them into reading experi-ences that sometimes repel and frustrate them. They are not yet adults. They are not ready for adult con-cerns. They have no background of experience to aid them in interpreting great adult literature. If we truly want our children someday to appreciate the classics, we must build reading ladders towards this goal. We can best accomplish this by allowing the young peo-ple's tastes to mature and mellow at their own pace. When they have learned to enjoy, savor, react, to the best of contemporary literature, they will be ready and eager to meet that great and wonderful body of clas-sics waiting just beyond their present reading horizon.

Bibliography

A compilation of books in poetry and prose spanning more than thirty-three centuries of man's most significant yearnings.

THE ANCIENT WORLD

The Bible, *See:*
 The Anchor Bible, Doubleday.
 The Bible Designed to Be Read as Living Literature, Earnest S. Bates, ed., Simon and Schuster.
 The Bible and the Common Reader, Mary Ellen Chase and others, eds., Macmillan.
 The Family and the Bible, Mary Reed Newland, ed., Random.
 The Modern King James Version of the Holy Bible. Teenage version, Green, ed., McGraw.
 The New Testament in Modern English, J. M. Phillips, ed., Macmillan.
Aeschylus: *Agamemnon.* The tragic drama of a man torn by the loyalties and responsibilities of ruler, soldier, and husband. Several editions.
———: *Prometheus Bound.* In a sense both thief and soothsayer, a young man attempts to mediate between the gods, heaven, and earthly need. See Edith Hamilton, *Three Greek Plays.* Norton, Oxford.
Euripides: *Medea.* The drama of a wife and mother who in seeking revenge proves how fine is the line between love and hate. See the translation by M. W. B. Townsend–Chandler.
Homer: *Iliad.* Detailed account of Achilles' retreat toward the end of the Trojan War. See the translation by Richmond Lattimore, University of Chicago Press.
———: *Odyssey.* The epic tale of Ulysses' homeward journey at the conclusion of the Trojan War. See the translation by W. H. D. Rouse, NAL.
Plato: *The Republic.* Socrates' dialogues on justice, order, and the individual.

Sophocles: *Antigone*. The tragic drama depicting a conflict between filial love and royal decree which results in death for those involved. See the translation by Gilbert Murray. Oxford.

————: *Oedipus Rex*. Man's blindness is shown in this drama as the hero tries to escape the fate prophesied by the Delphic oracle and brings disaster to his family and country by his actions.

See also:

Hamilton, Edith: *Mythology*. Little, Brown, 1942; Univ. Library; NAL. A most readable retelling of the ancient Greek myths that have become a part of Western culture.

————: *The Greek Way*. Norton, 1942. One of the best interpretations of ancient Greek civilization for the general reader.

BRITISH CLASSICS

(The date given is that of the first manuscript or of publication. Most of these classics are available in several editions.)

Austen, Jane: *Pride and Prejudice*. 1813. Social falsity and a too-great reliance on appearances are corrected in time to assure two marriages.

Bronte, Charlotte: *Jane Eyre*. 1847. A dark mystery stands between a shy governess and the unconventional employer whom she loves.

Bronte, Emily: *Wuthering Heights*. 1847. A London waif accepts a family's affections, only to repay them in later years with heartbreak.

Bunyan, John: *Pilgrim's Progress (From this World to that Which Is to Come)*. 1678–1684. An allegory tracing a young man's odyssey from the City of Destruction to the Gate of Heaven.

Butler, Samuel: *The Way of All Flesh*. 1903. The son of a clergyman, hampered by his parents and an unwise marriage, seeks self-respect.

Carroll, Lewis (Charles Lutwidge Dodgson): *Alice's Adventures in Wonderland*. 1865. A young girl literally falls into a world of fantastic make believe. See facsimile editions by Dover and University Microfilms.

Chaucer, Geoffrey: *Canterbury Tales*. c. 1395. Life and thought in medieval England are portrayed through a series of entertaining stories told by imaginary pilgrims on the way to Canterbury.

Conrad, Joseph: *Lord Jim.* 1900. A young seaman commits an act of cowardice and spends the rest of his life struggling to atone for this error and to regain his self-respect.

————: *The Secret Sharer.* 1912. In his first command a ship's captain is faced with a crucial decision that will affect his own life and that of a murderer.

Defoe, Daniel: *Robinson Crusoe.* 1720. An island castaway and his native companion mix ingenuity and adventure in making for themselves a civilized life.

Dickens, Charles: *David Copperfield.* 1850. Despite cruel treatment as a child, a young man achieves success and happiness in this novel most noted for its memorable secondary characters.

————: *Great Expectations.* 1861. Pip's life is changed by a strange circumstance. He grows to manhood expecting a great inheritance and marriage with his childhood sweetheart. Neither is fulfilled.

————: *A Tale of Two Cities.* 1859. Charles Darnay is convicted by the French Revolutionists for a crime of his ancestors and is sentenced to the guillotine. He is saved by his friend, Sidney Carton.

Eliot, George (Mary Anne Evans): *Mill on the Floss.* 1860. A brother and sister are tied together by both affection and a tragic accident.

Galsworthy, John: *The Forsyte Saga.* 1906–1921. A trilogy which depicts the materialism and confused affections in the life of a "successful" London family.

Goldsmith, Oliver: *She Stoops to Conquer.* 1773. Charles Marlowe. a shy suitor, is tricked into a series of errors, but wins the young heiress in spite of them.

————: *The Vicar of Wakefield.* 1776. A series of turns, both tragic and fortunate, punctuates the life of a gentle, gullible clergyman and his family.

Hardy, Thomas: *The Mayor of Casterbridge.* 1884. A successful businessman in an English country town is tumbled from his position by his past.

————: *Tess of the D'Urbervilles.* 1891. An essentially good woman is brought to tragedy because she bore an illegitimate child.

Hudson, William Henry: *Green Mansions.* 1904. Romance and untimely loss in the South American jungles. Powerfully descriptive.

Kipling, Rudyard: *Kim.* 1901. A young Irish boy, afoot in colonial India, is involved both with a native mystic and
with the Secret Service.

Malory, Sir Thomas: *Morte d'Arthur.* 1468. The life of King
Arthur and related legends.

Scott, Sir Walter: *Ivanhoe.* 1819. A romance of chivalry and
intrigue set in the time of Richard the Lion-Hearted and
Robin Hood.

Shakespeare: William: *Complete Works of Shakespeare*—Player's Illustrated Edition, George Lyman Kittredge, ed.
Ginn, 1958. Authoritative introductions to each play, pho-
tographs of actual productions, and reliable text make
this an excellent choice for the person seeking all the.
plays in one book. Paperback editions of individual plays
are numerous.

Stevenson, Robert Louis: *The Strange Case of Dr. Jekyll and
Mr. Hyde.* 1886. Early science-fiction dealing with man's
goodness, his latent evil, and his transformation by drugs.

————: *Treasure Island.* 1883. A young boy narrates this colorful tale of pirates, buried treasure, and a nearly successful mutiny.

Swift, Jonathan: *Gulliver's Travels.* 1726. A satirical fantasy
of Gulliver's capture by the tiny Lilliputians and later by
the gigantic Brobdingnags. Finally he lives with the
Houyhnhnms, rational horses who are the masters of irrational human beings. Avoid the cut or incomplete versions.

Thackeray, William Makepeace: *Vanity Fair.* 1848. Becky
Sharp, an ambitious woman, moves up the social scale
through her wits. Set in early nineteenth-century London.

Wells, H. G.: *Tono-Bungay.* 1909. The fortune derived from
a patent medicine assures two men quite different brands
of success.

————: *The War of the Worlds.* 1898. A Martian invasion
which, in a 1938 radio adaptation, caused real panic
throughout the United States.

Wilde, Oscar: *The Importance of Being Earnest.* 1895. The
comical narration of a young man's rise in fortune once
he solves the mystery of his paternity.

————: *The Picture of Dorian Gray.* 1891. A young man's
moral degeneration is strangely and faithfully chronicled
in his portrait.

WORLD CLASSICS

(The date given is that of the first complete manuscript or
of publication.)

Cervantes (Saavedra), Miguel de: *Don Quixote.* 1615. An attempt to recapture chivalry and romance transforms the
life of an angular country gentleman. See Leighton Bar-
ret's edition for junior high readers (Knopf).

Chekhov, Anton Pavlovich: *The Cherry Orchard.* 1904. A
once wealthy family, unable to cope with the onslaught
of time, loses both pride and property in this Russian
drama.

Dante (Alighieri): *The Divine Comedy.* 1321. An epic, allegory, and critique in which the poet traces a detailed
passage through hell and heaven. See the translation by
John Ciardi (Rutgers), Joseph Tusiani, *Dante's Inferno
as Told for Young people* (Obolensky).

Dostoevsky, Fyodor: *The Brothers Karamazov.* 1880. A many-
sided narrative which defines complex relationships among
a father and his four sons.

———: *Crime and Punishment.* 1866. A detailed psychological study of a young man's crime, guilt, and ultimate
contrition.

Dumas, Alexandre: *The Count of Monte Cristo.* 1844. Politics,
imprisonment, escape, discovery, and retribution mark the
life of a mysterious stranger.

———: *The Three Musketeers.* 1844. The friendship and
adventurous exploits of four young swordsmen in seven-
teenth-century France.

Flaubert, Gustave: *Madame Bovary.* 1856. Boredom and un-
happiness lay siege to a pathetic, discontented wife of
a country doctor.

Gibran, Kahlil: *The Prophet.* Knopf, 1923. Poetic prose statements of mysticism and deep religious commitment.

Goethe, Johann Wolfgang von: *The Sorrows of Young Werther.*
1787. A young romantic becomes hopelessly entangled in
his own speculations.

Hugo, Victor: *Les Misérables.* 1862. The theft of a loaf of
bread plagues the life and fortunes of a man who struggles
for dignity.

Ibsen, Henrik: *A Doll's House*. 1879. In this Scandinavian play, a woman, overprotected throughout her life, discovers she must make a clean break with all she has known in order to discover her own capabilities.

————: *Hedda Gabler*. 1890. A drama of an ambitious young woman who attempts to control the destinies of two men by a series of unsuccessful intrigues.

Khayyám, Omar: *The Rubáiyát*. 1460. (translated by Edward FitzGerald). A series of Persian quatrains dwelling on the beauties and satisfactions of a sensual life.

Molière (Jean Baptiste Poquelin): *The Misanthrope and Other Plays*. Sharply incisive comedies dealing with human pretension.

Rostand, Edmond: *Cyrano de Bergerac*. 1897. In this remarkable play a dashing poet and would-be lover encounters problems because of his long nose.

Stendhal (Henri Beyle). *The Red and the Black*. 1830. The highly psychological novel of an ambitious young man and his search for power.

Tolstoi, Count Leo: *Anna Karenina*. 1875. Two love matches are contrasted in this study of a young woman's inability to accept life as it is.

————: *War and Peace*. 1877. The Napoleonic War and the lives of many people, both foolish and wise, are interwoven in this monumental work.

Voltaire: *Candide*. 1759. An unlikely series of misadventures leads a young man to doubt his tutor's belief that all is for the best.

CLASSICS OF AMERICAN LITERATURE

(The date given is that of the first complete manuscript or of publication. Most of these classics are available in several editions.)

Bellamy, Edward: *Looking Backward*. 1888. Bostonians are transported into the future—a socialist state in the year 2000.

Cooper, James Fenimore: *The Last of the Mohicans*. 1826. The French and Indian War is the background of the romantic story of Indian-white man relations in the forests of New York.

Crane, Stephen: *The Open Boat and Other Stories*. Harper.

Impressionist-realist stories of man in conflict both with
nature and with himself.

————: *The Red Badge of Courage.* 1895. A study of fear as
it affects the life and romantic presuppositions of a young
Union soldier in the Civil War.

Hawthorne, Nathaniel: *The House of the Seven Gables.* 1851.
For 200 years the Pyncheon family has suffered from the
curse laid on their house, but young Phoebe Pyncheon
falls in love and dispels the curse.

————: *The Scarlet Letter.* 1850. This story explores both on
a literal and a symbolic level the effect on a Puritan community of Hester Prynne's adultery. Guilt, evil, courage,
are the dark components of the story.

Howells, William Dean: *The Rise of Silas Lapham.* 1885. A
successful Boston merchant develops ethical standards
while accumulating a short-lived wealth.

James, Henry: *The American.* 1877. Contrasts between simplicity and sophistication are developed in this novel of an
American in nineteenth-century Paris.

————: *The Portrait of a Lady.* Scribners, 1917; Wash. Sq.
Isabel Archer, a wealthy young American, weds an English
dilettante in her hope of finding the best of men and ideas
abroad. James incisively contrasts American and British
types and social mores.

London, Jack: *The Sea Wolf.* 1904. During a long sea voyage
a young man is shanghaied into service by a ruthless
captain.

————: *Martin Eden.* Holt, 1909. A young writer discovers
that success assures "friendships" of which failure only
dreams.

Melville, Herman: *Billy Budd.* 1851. Impressed into sea service, Billy Budd finds his youthful innocence sharply contrasted by the evil of the Master-at-Arms. When he strikes
down his persecutor, he meets with swift maritime justice.

————: *Moby Dick.* 1851. A strange sea captain involves his
crew in a mystical pursuit of the great white whale, Moby
Dick. The narrator alone survives.

Norris, Frank: *The Octopus.* 1901. California ranching and rail-
road interests are presented in an intense power struggle.

Poe, Edgar Allan: *Short Stories.* Poe is a master at detailing
inner and imagined horror.

Sinclair, Upton: *The Jungle.* 1906; Airmont; Signet. Set in
Chicago of the early 1900's, this story shows the terrible
labor conditions and exploitation in the stockyards.

Stowe, Harriet Beecher: *Uncle Tom's Cabin*. 1852. A significant abolitionist document, this novel delineates the horrible conditions of the Negro under slavery.

Thoreau, Henry David: *Walden*. 1854. Chronicle of the author's two-year search for values as he lived alone at the edge of Walden pond.

Twain, Mark (Samuel Langhorne Clemens): *The Adventures of Tom Sawyer*. 1876. The free and easy life of a boy in Hannibal, Missouri, at the end of the nineteenth century.

————: *The Adventures of Huckleberry Finn*. 1884. Huck Finn runs away with an escaped slave and makes a long trip on a raft down the Mississippi River. This is one of the greatest American novels.

————: *A Connecticut Yankee in King Arthur's Court*. 1889. The satiric misadventures of a man who finds himself transported backward in time.

————: *The Prince and the Pauper*. 1881. Two boys exchange roles for a brief and revealing education.

Wharton, Edith N. J.: *Ethan Frome*. Scribners, 1911. A reversal of personalities marks this ironic novel of a triangle love affair in a New England village.

————: *The Age of Innocence*. 1920; Signet. Conflict between love and convention in the New York society of the 1870 s.

Chapter 10
Poetry

Poetry is the silence and speech between a wet struggling
root of a flower and sunlit blossom of that flower.
Carl Sandburg

We live in an age of prose, not of poetry, and our culture has undoubtedly affected the reading habits and
preferences of the present generation. The bulk of our
published literature for the past two hundred years
has been prose. Yet we know that poetry is a natural
form of expression for human beings. Delight in the
rhythmic arrangements of words is as old as man's
communication itself. In the long history of mankind,
poetry has been the most common form of literary expression. The great historical traditions are embedded
in such poetic epics as the *Iliad*, the *Ramayana*, the
Kalevala. For hundreds of years, until prose came into
its own around the eighteenth century, man used
poetry to express his ideas and to interpret the events
in his life. There is, then, nothing about poetry that
makes it "unnatural" and nothing inherent in its form
or content that makes it more difficult to comprehend
than prose. However, since we live in an age in which
we are conditioned to prose literature, few people,
either adults or adolescents, devote long periods of
time to reading poetry for sheer pleasure.

Most persons do read poetry at certain times. It may
be only a casual glance as they thumb through a cur-

rent magazine and their eye falls on a poem that they skim before turning the page. It may happen while they are browsing through a shelf of books and the thin, beautifully bound volume lures them to glance inside because of its rich appearance. Or it may be while hunting for a poem to use for a Thanksgiving program. Or it may be when they are preparing an assignment for a class at school and find that reading one poem leads to another. Frequently the impact of a poem is way out of proportion to the amount of time devoted to reading it. A remembered line from a poem helps one interpret a moment of beauty, a feeling about a particular person, the reaction to birth or growing up or death, to the change of the seasons, the rhythms of daily existence. There are times when a person would be lost indeed if he could not dip into the reservoir of images brought to life by the poets.

So although the total amount of poetry that an individual may read in a lifetime will continue to be small in quantity when compared to prose, it is of tremendous importance. Certainly the child who has grown up with a generous exposure to poetry in his background will be the richer for it.

Certain cultures and particular periods of history have been more richly endowed with the gift of poetry than have others. One of the richest and most steady outpourings of poetry has come from the British Isles. The English—strait-laced, unsentimental, dignified, a nation of merchants, sailors, industrialists—seem hardly the stuff from which poets spring. And yet for a thousand years they have produced hundreds of great poets. They reached their peak during two eras: the one occurred in the sixteenth and early seventeenth centuries in the period ruled over by Elizabeth I, and the second during the whole of the nineteenth century.

Benefiting from this rich poetic heritage American poetry has flourished. Since the nineteenth century in New England, American poets have substantially con-

tributed to contemporary writing. Many of the stimulating ideas about our culture today and man's relationship to it are expressed by the prolific and vibrant
poets of our own generation.

There are four or five standard collections of English poetry which present well-selected samplings from
the reservoir of our poetic tradition. They skim off the
best for the young reader who may be just starting to
become interested, but they are comprehensive enough
to include particular poems he may be assigned in
class. The fashion for this kind of collection was set in
1861 by a professor in England, Francis T. Palgrave.
He set out with Lord Tennyson and other literary
friends to winnow out the best lyric poems written in
English after 1550. He was interested in individually
fine poems, not in poets. His preferences and tastes
have proved to be remarkably enduring, for Palgrave's
Golden Treasury has become almost a "must" in most
libraries. Though Professor Palgrave died over sixty
years ago, his collection has since been edited and
added to by astute and able persons. It still remains a
fine, standard collection of English verse organized in
a chronological pattern.

The Oxford Book of English Verse is a larger standard collection. It has the advantage of sampling both
English and American poetry. For the family library
it serves as a single-volume collection of a large body
of the poems that a student may be looking for, as
well as a volume in which to browse and make discoveries for himself. A similar excellent collection is
Stevenson's *Home Book of Verse;* it gives a reader a
taste of the best of the poetry of English-speaking
peoples.

While it is important that the young reader have
access to the body of standard poetry, perhaps when
a sudden mood moves him to find out "what this
poetry stuff is all about,"—he will at first find light
verse more fun. In a survey conducted among high

school students by the University of Iowa, young people revealed a good deal about what they really wanted in poetry. First and foremost they cast their votes for humorous verse. They wanted nonsense rhymes. It is all too true that in most schools the poetry presented tends to be pretty serious. In the words of one boy, "There is too much stuff about clouds and daffodils."

To satisfy this interest in lighthearted rhymes, William Cole has collected some five hundred pages of delightfully funny verse in *The Fireside Book of Humorous Poetry*. Most of it is modern. It tickles one's funny bone through its incongruities, a ridiculous rhyme, an unexpected or concocted word, an unusual pattern of rhythm. The poems are organized around such themes as "The Other Animals," "Bores and Boors," "Races, Places, and Dialects," "In Praise and Dispraise of Love." Once a reader dips into this book he will feel compelled to keep turning the pages so he can read the next ridiculous poem.

A perennial favorite form of humorous verse is the limerick. The limerick is a five-line form in which the first, second, and last lines rhyme. The third and fourth lines rhyme with each other. This pattern seems to lend itself to zany combinations of ideas. One of the most delightful collections of limericks is Bennett Cerf's *Out on a Limerick*, which he calls a collection of the "world's best printable limericks," and he assures the reader that they have been "dry-cleaned." The volume opens with ten of the best known limericks. Then come ten by the originator of the form, Edward Lear. After these, the limericks are grouped around such subjects as "Love and Marriage," "Near and Distant Places," "Fun with Names," and the like.

Probably Ogden Nash and Richard Armour have amused more readers than any other two living poets. Nash is the master of long sentences that are bizarrely arranged on the page, and of the outrageous manipulation of words to make the ridiculous and unexpected rhyme. Richard Armour's forte, on the other hand, is poking fun at literary, historical and modern personalities with quick, witty thrusts.

While adolescents *say* that they like humorous poetry best, when asked to list their favorite poems, narrative poems always come out on top. Recently a group of teen-agers selected as their favorites such titles as "The Highwayman," "The Raven," "Casey at the Bat," "The Cremation of Sam McGee," "Paul Revere's Ride," "The Rhyme of the Ancient Mariner." The tremendous interest in folk singing of the present generation springs from the human impulse to tell and listen to a story, in verse. The novice balladeer begins with the familiar, well-known folk songs that have sifted down from one generation to the next. But the sophisticated, modern balladeer does what all great folk singers have done through the ages: he sings of the events of his own times—racial integration, political issues, contemporary wars, burnings and marches, tragedies in human life. The ballad has always been an instrument of social criticism—a way for the man on the street to express his indignation at the events in his culture which are controlled by a few status figures.

Because of this vital interest in storytelling poems, it is important to provide the young reader with at least one standard collection of folk ballads. MacEdward Leach's *The Ballad Book* is an excellent collection. It contains 250 English, Scotch, and American ballads with variant forms of the same ballad. This is a good source book for the budding folk singer who frequently wants the words to some old standard folk song. It also provides the youngsters not interested in performing with fast-moving stories whose action is heightened by the use of rhythm and rhyme. *The Ballad of America,* a paperback anthology edited by John Anthony Scott, shows how folk songs have expressed the traditions and experiences of the American people.

Elinor Parker has made two popular collections of storytelling poems. One called *100 Story Poems* is a balanced selection of the most familiar of the old ballads, some of the best of the nineteenth-century narrative poems and a few modern pieces such as "Dunkirk." The stories are grouped by themes such as "Poems about History," "Poems about the Sea," "Kings, Knights, and Heroes." The second collection, *100 More Story Poems*, contains less familiar narrative poems. It is somewhat easier than the first and hence more suitable for younger readers.

William Cole has sought out many of the less well known story poems for his book *Story Poems New and Old*. He leans heavily on narrative poems by American authors and uses a nice mixture of serious and humorous selections. The simplicity of the poems makes this an excellent collection for junior high school readers.

Perhaps it is a commentary on the times that there are few book-length narrative poems written about contemporary subjects. The long poem seems to have passed with the Victorians. Unfortunately most of their favorites such as *The Lady of the Lake, Evangeline*, or *The Idylls of the King* all have a Victorian style that most adolescent readers categorically reject. To be sure, an occasional romantically inclined young reader may find great pleasure in such poems, but this is not the usual reaction. Perhaps the best long narrative poem by a relatively contemporary poet is *John Brown's Body*, by Stephen Vincent Benét. Here is poetry of real stature that tells the story of the Civil War through the experiences of two young men, one from the North and one from the South. The story is so vivid that the reader often forgets that he is reading poetry although the emotional impact is certainly increased by the fact that the story is expressed in poetic form. Another fairly modern narrative poem is

Agnes Duer Miller's *White Cliffs of Dover* which had
a wave of popularity during the years of the Second
World War. It tells the modern story of an American
woman who falls in love and marries an Englishman
who is killed in the First World War; she then finds
history repeating itself with her son in the Second
World War. Such book-length narratives in poetry are
worth seeking and including in your library.

Since literature always reflects the problems of contemporary life, modern verse is frequently the most
significant poetry for the adolescent. Poetry of the past
seems often to encompass only a relatively few basic
subjects: love, nature, and religion. But modern poetry
is not bound by such narrow limits: it runs the whole
range of modern life from automobile wrecks to astro-
nauts, from disassembling guns and motorcycle
rumbles to heroism in battle and praising of God.
Whitman expressed the spirit of modern poetry when
he talked of sounding his "barbaric yawp over the
rooftops of the world." So today's poetry experiments
with both language and content. To the uninitiated it
often seems as confused and barbaric as modern life
itself.

Poets in every age have experimented, and what
seems strange in one age becomes commonplace in
the next. It is well to remember that when Coleridge
and Byron and Shelley and Wordworth were first published they were considered unpoetic and incompre-
hensible by the staid readers of the period. And the
Victorians were not at all sure that Browning was
quite respectable. Hence poetry that seems obscure
and modern for one generation will probably seem
utterly simple to the next. The chances are good that
the adolescent reader has less difficulty making sense
out of today's verse than do his teachers and parents.

There are, of course, collections of modern poetry.
Two of the best are edited by Louis Untermeyer:
Modern American Poetry and *Modern British Poetry*.

These are available in two separate volumes, or in a single volume combined. There is also a shortened version of each intended for use in the secondary schools. The American volume starts with Walt Whitman, and the British volume begins with Thomas Hardy. The verse is arranged by poet, and the poets are placed in a roughly chronological sequence, beginning in the nineteenth century and coming down to the present time. A more selective anthology is *Mid-Century American Poets*, edited by John Ciardi, who chose poetry from a dozen contemporary poets most of whom are still actively writing.

Poetry by its very nature is something to be savored, to be read slowly, to be enjoyed. One does not read a book of poetry through from beginning to end in one sitting as one may read a novel. Rather the reader dips into such books, thumbing idly through the pages until a certain poem demands his attention. One's pleasure in poetry lies in the words and the very sounds they make, in the visions they present. Enjoyment may also be enhanced by the beauty of the book itself. Somehow it seems proper for poetry books to be thin, the paper heavy, and the print on the page so placed that one's eye is attracted to the lines. Fortunately recent years have seen the publication of many such small and delightful volumes for the adolescent reader. Many are specialized collections of poetry. The following are a few examples of possible choices.

Helen Plotz's collections have been unusually successful both in selection and in appearance. *Imagination's Other Place* is a group of poetry that deals only with the subject of science. There is nice balance of old poems and modern poems. The selections are grouped by such topics as "The Beginning," "The Kingdom of Number," "Watchers of the Skies." A second volume, *Untune the Sky*, centers on poetry that celebrates music and the dance. *The Earth Is The Lord's* brings together poetry describing the religious experience. Its subsections, ranging from "The Vision Splendid" to "Praise Doubt," indicate the wide range of religious thinking presented.

William Cole is another editor who has brought together short collections of poetry of a specialized nature. *The Birds and the Beasts Were There* is a really distinguished group of poems about animals. The editor has avoided the pitfall of many such collections by eliminating the precious and sentimental which dominate so much animal poetry. Neither are the poems grade-schoolish in tone. Another of Cole's good collections is *Poems for Seasons and Celebrations,* which is organized chronologically from New Year's Day to Christmas. Here is a good place to find a poem to be used for a seasonal program or for a holiday theme that a teen-ager is assigned. The same editor has also put together *A Book of Love Poems,* which succeeds in avoiding the banal and presents love in the words of distinguished poets as a "many splendored thing."

This Way, Delight, edited by Herbert Read and illustrated by Juliet Kepes, is a lovely book of lyrics. Its poetry captures those little will o' the wisp thoughts and feelings that are the glory and excitement of poetry. Padraic Colum's *Roofs of Gold* is a handsome book of poems intended for reading aloud. *Poems for Pleasure* is a popular collection edited by Herman Ward, a teacher who worked with his own tenth- and eleventh-grade students in class and in groups at his home. He read them a great many poems and allowed them to make the selections for the book. This volume really represents adolescent tastes. The collection has great variety, ranging from "Barefoot Boy" and "The Cremation of Sam McGee" to Keats's "Ode on a Grecian Urn."

There are, of course, many volumes devoted to the works of a single poet. In general, outside of the works of the humorists like Ogden Nash or Richard Armour, few young people have sufficiently developed tastes to settle down with a whole book by one writer. They prefer an anthology that allows them to dip into the poetry of many different writers.

Poetry is certainly not indispensable to human life, but it is a source of rich pleasure and gives a heightened awareness to the nuances of living. Therefore it seems well worth helping your son or daughter to discover this form of expression. Life is always deepened and enriched when one can find the exact words to capture the essence of a moment. To be able to use the language of poetry to express a reaction is immensely rewarding: to think of that blue and gold fall day as "the season of mellow fruitfulness"; of the soft winter snowfall as "a walk with velvet shoes"; of the restless drive of men as the restlessness "of a motorcycle rumble." Somehow the words of the poets increase our own awareness and our understanding of ourselves and of the moment.

It is doubtful in our age of prose that the adolescent, except for the exceptional one, will seek out poetry for himself. But a parent can see that there are four or five books of poetry around the house. Although the amount of poetry read will probably always be small, its impact can be far out of proportion to its quantity.

Bibliography

GENERAL COLLECTIONS OF POETRY

Auslander, Joseph, and Frank Hill, eds.: *The Winged Horse Anthology*. Doubleday, 1929. An old favorite among students and teachers as a source for the best of traditional poetry. Poems are arranged chronologically from Chaucer

and medieval ballads to modern poets, such as Robert
Frost and Carl Sandburg.

Bogan, Louise, and William Jay Smith, eds.: *The Golden Journey: Poems for Young People*. Reilly and Lee, 1965. A
collection of poems "fresh, delightful, and perennially
new."

Creekmore, Hubert, ed.: *A Little Treasury of World Poetry*.
Scribners, 1952. Translations into English of outstanding
poetry written in foreign languages dating back to earliest
Babylonian hymns. Arranged by language and chronologically by author within each language.

Niebling, Richard F., ed.: *A Journey of Poems*. Dell, 1964. An
original paperback for young people, including poems by
Pope, Tennyson, Frost, Byron, Auden, and others.

Palgrave, Francis T., ed.: *The Golden Treasury*. Oxford, 1964;
rev. Mentor. First published in 1861, but still maintains
its freshness and usefulness. Though it included no selections by living poets at the time of its publication, most
modern editions have selections from later poets. Revised
by Oscar Williams.

Quiller-Couch, Arthur, ed.: *The Oxford Book of English Verse*.
Oxford, 1939, rev. 1957. Classics of British and American
poetry from 1250 to 1918 arranged chronologically by
author.

Warren, Robert Penn, and Albert Erskine, eds.: *Six Centuries
of Great Poetry*. Dell, 1955. More than one hundred poets
are represented in this collection of the greatest English
lyric poetry from Chaucer to Yeats.

LARGE COLLECTIONS OF POETRY FOR BROWSING

Adshead, Gladys, and Annis Duff, eds.: *An Inheritance of
Poetry*. Houghton, 1948. A collection of simple imaginative
poems in the lyric mode for families who like to read and
sing together. Includes an index to musical settings. Poems
are grouped by similarity of mood with no editorial comment.

De La Mare, Walter, ed.: *Come Hither*. Knopf, 1960. Collection ranging from nursery rhymes and jingles to sophisticated verse, with an antiquarian interest in the quaint,
the picturesque and the gnomic. Organized under seventeen themes such as "Morning and May"; "Elphin, Ouph
and Fay"; "War"; "Old Tales and Ballads."

Gannett, Lewis, S., ed.: *The Family Book of Verse*. Harper, 1961. Organized by themes such as "Notes of Ecstasy"; "Sounds of the Sea"; "Our Other Eden." Concentrates on poetry that is to be read, not studied.

Stevenson, Burton Egbert, ed.: *The Home Book of Verse*. Holt, 1953. An older and very large standardized collection of favorite poetry arranged topically.

COLLECTIONS OF MODERN POETRY

Aiken, Conrad, ed.: *Twentieth-Century American Poetry*. Mod. Lib., 1963. Compact volume of carefully chosen poems which represent many different types of modern poetry.

Ciardi, John, ed.: *Mid-Century American Poets*. Twayne, 1950. Selections of a dozen contemporary poets such as Richard Wilbur, Robert Lowell, Elizabeth Bishop, and Ciardi himself with introductory statements from the poets about their own writing.

Rodman, Selden, ed.: *One Hundred Modern Poems*. Mentor, 1961. A sampling of the best modern poetry in this paperback edition.

Stevenson, Burton Egbert, ed.: *The Home Book of Modern Verse*. Holt, 1953. An extension of *Home Book of Verse*, devoted to contemporary verse written for the most part in traditional rhythms and forms.

Untermeyer, Louis, ed.: *Modern American Poetry and Modern British Poetry*. Harcourt, 1962. Actually two books in one, this selection by one of the best known anthologists of the age is becoming the standard in its field. Also available in other editions including a shorter high school version, *The New Modern American and The New Modern British Poetry*.

Williams, Oscar, ed.: *A Pocket Book of Modern Verse*. Wash. Sq., rev. 1960. From Walt Whitman to Dylan Thomas, more than five hundred English and American poems.

HUMOROUS POETRY

Cerf, Bennett, ed.: *Out on a Limerick*. Harper, 1960; Pocket. "Collection of over 300 of the world's best printable limericks."

Cole, William, ed.: *The Fireside Book of Humorous Poetry*. Simon and Schuster, 1959. A big collection of well-selected, humorous verse.

Nash, Ogden, ed.: *The Moon Is Shining Bright as Day*. Lippincott, 1953. Modern humorous verse ranging from slapstick to simple satire and parody.

Wells, Carolyn, ed.: *A Nonsense Anthology*. Dover, 1958. Delightful paperback collection of poems just for fun.

STORYTELLING POETRY

Causley, Charles, ed.: *Modern Ballads and Story Poems*. Watts, 1965. New and unfamiliar narrative poems. In the tradition of folk ballads, they often deal with the unknown, the unexpected, and the mysterious.

Cole, William, ed.: *Story Poems New and Old*. World Pub., 1957. Serious and humorous poetry drawn primarily from American poets. Appropriate at the junior high level.

Leach, MacEdward, ed.: *The Ballad Book*. Harper, 1955. 250 English, Scottish, and American ballads with variant forms.

Parker, Elinor, ed.: *100 Story Poems*. Crowell, 1951. Excellent collection ranging from some old ballads and nineteenth-century narrative favorites to a few modern ones.

————: *100 More Story Poems*. Crowell, 1960. Less well-known narrative poems than in the above book. Suitable for youngsters of junior high age.

SINGLE LONG NARRATIVE POEMS

Benét, Stephen Vincent: *John Brown's Body*. Holt, 1928. Best known poem about the American Civil War, its events and its people.

Miller, Alice Duer: *White Cliffs of Dover*. Coward, 1940. American woman faces her son's going into the Second World War after having lost her husband in the First World War.

Stoutenburg, Adrien: *Heroes, Advise Us*. Scribners, 1964; Scribners. Includes "This Journey," the narrative of Robert F. Scott's fatal expedition to the South Pole, where he had been preceded by Roald Amundsen.

COLLECTIONS FOR SPECIALIZED INTERESTS

Bennett, George, and Paul Molloy, eds.: *Cavalcade of Poems.* Scholastic, 1965. A selection of poems organized thematically, selected by students and the editors. In paper.

Cole, William, ed.: *The Birds and the Beasts Were There.* World, 1963. Distinguished collection of poetry about animals. Avoids the precious and the childish in favor of a wide variety of poems about the unusual and the commonplace, the whimsical and the symbolic in the animal kingdom.

————: *A Book of Love Poems.* Viking, 1965. Old favorite poems in this modern context resume their freshness and sincerity. None of the triteness and sentimentality that so often characterize books of poetry about love. Two unusual sections are "He Writes about Her" and "She Writes About Him."

————: *Poems for Seasons and Celebrations.* World, 1961. Follows the year from New Year's to Christmas with all the seasons and major holidays represented, as well as a few surprises such as Ground Hog Day and April Fools' Day.

Colum, Padraic, ed.: *Roofs of Gold.* Macmillan, 1964. Poems to be read aloud chosen from the viewpoint that poems should be "earned" and not "learned." Beautifully illustrated with woodcuts by Thomas Bewick.

Gregory, Horace, and Marya Zaturenska, eds.: *The Crystal Cabinet: An Invitation to Poetry.* Holt, 1962. Like the poem by William Blake from which the title is taken, these are poems of insight and intuition, most of which have not appeared frequently in other anthologies.

Hannum, Sara, and Gwendolyn Reed, eds.: *Lean Out of the Window.* Atheneum, 1965. Unusual collection of little known lyrics from well known modern poets such as James Joyce, T. S. Eliot, and Wallace Stevens.

Hughes, Langston, ed.: *New Negro Poets: U.S.A.* Indiana Univ., 1964. Sensitive poems of love, poems of bitter protest, poems of everyday life, written by young Negro poets.

————, and Arna Bontemps, eds.: *The Poetry of the Negro, 1746–1949.* Doubleday, 1949. Includes both poets in the

United States and in the Caribbean and tributary poems
by non-Negroes.

McDonald, Gerald D., comp.: *A Way of Knowing.* Crowell,
1959. Vigorous poetry especially for boys, organized
around such themes as "Fur, Fin, Feather"; "Live and
Learn"; and "O, Pioneers!"

Morrison, Lillian, ed.: *Sprints and Distances.* Crowell, 1965.
"The poetry of sports and the sport of poetry." Represents
almost all popular team and individual sports.

Plotz, Helen, ed.: *The Earth Is the Lord's.* Crowell, 1965.
Poems of the spirit. Tough, resilient, but inspiring poems
of faith and doubt, of brotherhood and sainthood.

————: *Imagination's Other Places.* Crowell, 1955. Poems of
science and mathematics, including astronomy, geography,
physics, mathematics, chemistry, biology, medicine and
tributes to men of science from Euclid to Einstein.

————: *Untune the Sky.* Crowell, 1957. Poems of music and
the dance from ancient to modern times.

Read, Herbert, ed.: *This Way, Delight.* Pantheon, 1956. Lovely
book of sensitive, will-o'-the-wisp thoughts and feelings.

Ward, Herman, ed.: *Poems for Pleasure.* Hill & Wang, 1963;
paper. Choices were made by the editor's tenth- and
eleventh-grade classes, which came to his home and lis-
tened to a great deal of poetry read aloud and discussed
it among themselves until they agreed on what should be
included. Organized in a "carefully disorganized fashion."

FOREIGN POETRY

Canfield, Kenneth, ed.: *Selections from French Poetry.* Harvey
House, 1965.

Jauss, Anne Marie, ed.: *Spanish American Poetry.* Harvey
House, 1964.

Resnick, Seymour, ed.: *Selections from Spanish Poetry.* Harvey
House, 1965. Each collection in this section has the original
on one page and the translation on the facing page.

Chapter 11
Biography—The Bridge Between Fact and Fiction

There is no such thing as a great man or a great woman. People believe in them, just as they used to believe in unicorns and dragons. The greatest man or woman is 99 per cent just like yourself.

George Bernard Shaw

Stories about people and what they have done are as old as mankind. Every group of people has constructed legends about its heroes, and such legends have their roots in fact. Even today social conversation often revolves around people and what they are doing: our own activities, those of a friend, or even the experiences of a friend of a friend. But most people like best to talk about the exploits of the great or near great in their world. Our newspapers and magazines give full coverage to a royal couple's visit to the United States, tell how the President celebrated Christmas, or report the reactions of a baseball star on the losing side of the World Series. It is out of this natural curiosity that we have about people, particularly the great people of the world, that biography springs. But biography satisfies more needs than simple curiosity. For the teen-ager this material may serve a variety of purposes.

Biographies often serve as a transition from fiction to nonfiction. In the early years of adolescence, young people prefer fiction to any other kind of reading material. The young reader likes a plot with such suspense that he is led uncritically and breathlessly from peak to peak. He likes exciting characters and a narrative line that follows a formula and permits easy skimming of the page rather than careful reading like the expository writing in his school texts. Biography shares the verve and movement of fiction, has as its center the actions and experiences of an exciting personality, and usually moves in a chronological order. But it shares with text materials a close attention to facts and details. Thus biography may give pertinent and true information about the social climate of an era, the details of a particular scientific investigation, the exploration of social ideas, the strange course of testing a scientific theory, the development of technological processes. Such material demands more careful reading than does fiction.

Secondly, biography may not only lead to nonfiction reading in general, but may help to widen an adolescent's interests. *The Walls of Windy Troy,* details the life of that strange man Heinrich Schliemann, who pioneered modern archaeology in his discovery of ancient Troy. Perhaps a reader who is intrigued by this book might decide to do further reading in the field of archaeology. At the same time, his interest in ancient Greek civilization might be stimulated.

A biography reveals how a person became interested in a particular field, how he pursued this interest, and ultimately what satisfaction he found in the process. In the biographies of scientists, for example, the young scientist can see what is meant by the scientific method and how a theory is tested, rejected, approved. All the byways, the blind alleys, the multitudinous possibilities that must be explored, are painstakingly detailed in the story of the Curies and their pursuit of radium.

Biography illuminates moments in history. If we read the life of Alexander the Great or Napoleon we will probably discover a great deal about the periods they lived in. Teen-agers actually do like to read about

many historical personalities. They love the success
stories of Julius Caesar, Abraham Lincoln, Booker T.
Washington, and John F. Kennedy. And at the same
time they learn about the Roman world, the Civil War,
an emancipated Negro's struggle for his rights, and
some recent American history.

Most human beings have someone whom they admire and whose image influences their dreams and
actions. Young people, in particular, are hero worship-
ers. In biography they can find the whole gamut of
great personalities to emulate. One adolescent reader
of a biography of Commander Perry found in him
everything he wanted to be himself. At sub-zero temperatures he took to sleeping on the floor in a sleeping
bag with his windows open wide. And so excited was
he by the idea of a career in arctic exploration that he
persuaded a university research team to sign him on
for a summer in the Arctic Circle. Not all young
readers react so completely to the challenge of a book
nor are they so successful in putting their dreams into
action. But for most, reading about a successful sports
figure, an accomplished dancer or scientist, or a dedicated missionary helps to clarify their needs and interests. It is deeply satisfying to see what human beings
"just like us" can do when they push themselves to
the limits of their strength and ability.

Some six or seven hundred new biographies are
published each year. Each one is appealing to particular readers because of certain specialized interests, but
only a very few out of each year's crop will have
enough appeal to achieve widespread readership and
critical acclaim.

In this mass of biographical material, those books
that will appeal to young adults have certain characteristics in common. On the basis of surveys set up at
the University of Iowa to determine their tastes, adolescents overwhelmingly demand that the writer make
the person come alive. This means that they will gen-

erally reject the so-called "definitive" biography in which the writer catalogues and presents all the factual information available. They prefer the "interpretive" biography in which the author finds the central threads of an individual's life that made him an interesting personality. Such a book will tend to be short (300 pages) rather than monumental (1,000 pages). And it will contain "imagined" conversations or "imagined" reactions which the author attributes to the character. In other words, the young people want their biography materials to have qualities similar to those of fiction.

As the subject of biographies, adolescents prefer the contemporary person. Girls sometimes gratify their romantic yearnings by reading biographies of queens and princesses, but they too prefer to read about the modern individual whose name currently appears in their newspapers. In the survey on biographies, the teen-age reader indicated that he had the greatest interest in the lives of scientists. The next most popular subject was the political figure. Boys had a more pronounced preference in these two areas than did girls. Boys also wanted to read about war heroes, while girls favored books about humanitarian figures and writers. These preferences indicate that the reading choices and personal interests of the adolescent are closely tied together.

How does one approach this mass of possible reading matter? One method is to introduce the young reader to short, one-chapter biographies. Although teen-agers seldom read a volume of collected biographies from cover to cover, there are many excellent collections of such biographies grouped by professions, historical periods, handicaps, a particular human quality, etc. Most familiar to modern readers is John F. Kennedy's *Profiles in Courage*. Kennedy selected eight outstanding Americans who had taken an unpopular point of view and stood by it. Through their courage they helped to define the concept of American democracy. In a book called *The Presidents in American History,* Charles A. Beard, an eminent American historian, presents in successive chapters each President of the United States, and attempts to show how each shaped the events of his time or was himself shaped by the events. In *Crusaders for Freedom,* Henry Steele Commager portrays such people as Tom Paine, Harriet Tubman, Elizabeth Blackwell and Jane Addams. Louis Untermeyer in *Makers of the Modern World* deals with a group of nineteenth- and twentieth-century figures in many different fields of human endeavor who helped create the world as we know it today: Darwin, Kierkegaard, Karl Marx, Mary Baker Eddy, Baudelaire, and T. S. Eliot are a few who are discussed. In *Twelve Citizens of the World,* Leonard Kenworthy gives well-rounded accounts of such people as Ralph Bunche, Mohandas K. Gandhi, Eleanor Roosevelt, and Albert Schweitzer. While most of these people are now dead, they still remain very much a part of the twentieth century.

There are many collections of biography to satisfy the student's interest in scientific figures. One of the best anthologies is the famous *Microbe Hunters,* by Paul de Kruif, the dramatic narrative of the discoveries of Leeuwenhoek, Pasteur, and Walter Reed. Among the newer collections are Sarah K. Bolton's *Famous Men of Science* and Lynn Poole's *Scientists Who Changed the World.* Such famous historical characters as Copernicus, Hippocrates, and Galileo are sketched, as well as modern scientists like Salk, Lee, Yang, and Freud.

Actually there are collections of short biographies in almost any field of interest. In sports one of the most arresting collections is Steve Gelman's *Young Olympic Champions* which tells the exciting stories of eleven athletes in their teens who won gold medals in the Olympics. The book also contains a listing of statistics on Olympic performances that many boys are eager to have.

Studs Terkel in *Giants of Jazz* has written a series of short biographies of figures in the jazz world such as Joe Oliver, Louis Armstrong, Fats Waller, and Woody Herman. *Titans of Business*, by Leonard M. Fanning, centers on a series of successful business people beginning with Alexander Hamilton and including such figures as J. P. Morgan, John D. Rockefeller, Sr., and Henry Ford I.

American writers have produced a number of book-length biographies especially written for the adolescent reader. The best of these authors try to make their presentation honest, exciting, and unified in total impression. In general, the material is fictionalized. This means that the writers imagine certain conversations and credit particular inner feelings to the characters. Some young adult biographies tend to gloss over or omit the most unsavory incidents in the lives of the famous. But most do clothe the people in flesh and blood and attribute human feelings and reactions to them in a compelling manner.

Five biographies have earned the Newbery Medal, awarded annually by the American Library Association for the book that has made the greatest contribution to young people's reading of a given year. One of these, *Carry on, Mr. Bowditch,* by Jean Lee Latham, tells the life story of the sailor who devised the manual for navigation which has been the Bible of sea captains since that day. Another, *Amos Fortune: Free Man*, by Elizabeth Yates, is the story of a Negro apprentice who eventually managed to buy his own freedom.

Among the authors who have specialized in writing biographies for the teen-age reader is Shannon Garst. She has concentrated on presenting Western heroes such as Sitting Bull, Crazy Horse, James Bowie, Jim Bridger, and Kit Carson. These historical figures are interesting to most boys at a particular time in their growth. Jeanette Eaton is another respected and productive writer in the biographical field. Her subjects range from Eleanor Roosevelt to Gandhi to Louis Armstrong. *Trumpeter's Tale* is a moving story depicting Armstrong's rise from poverty, his early jazz experiences in New Orleans, and his later experiments and contributions to modern music. J. Alvin Kugelmass also writes about a wide variety of people. Ralph Bunche and Roald Amundsen are the subjects of two of his books. Nina Baker, on the other hand, limits her biographical subjects to those political leaders in the world who contributed in some way to the struggle for human rights and dignity. Thus she gives young readers most readable accounts of people like Juarez, Simón Bolívar, Sun Yat-sen, and Garibaldi. She also wrote one of the few biographies of Lenin geared to the adolescent. Manuel Komroff has written books about Mozart, Julius Caesar, and Thomas Jefferson all of which use a simple vocabulary and yet maintain unity and depth of understanding that give dignity and maturity to the presentation. Elma Levinger has succeeded admirably in writing about two brilliant, esoteric people, Freud and Einstein, in such a way that she makes their basic concepts comprehensible.

There is also a group of books originally written for adult consumption but whose subject matter has such appeal for young people that they claim the books for their own. Such biographies often deal with relatively unknown people whose experiences are so unusual or so deeply personal in nature that the reader finds himself emotionally involved. For example, John Gunther's *Death Be Not Proud,* is a very short little book in which the author reconstructs the life of his son up to the age of sixteen when the boy died of a brain tumor. The reader feels the strange fortitude that strengthens the young man during the period of his illness, and he is deeply moved by the experience of the author as he must helplessly face the inevitable moment of death. Another such book is *Fifth Chinese Daughter*, the autobiography of Jade Snow Wong, a California ceramicist, who describes her experiences growing up in San Francisco's Chinatown. Here is a warm account of the conflict between generations to which the adolescent reader is peculiarly attuned. But the basic conflict is heightened by the circumstances. The foreign-born parents are desperately trying to maintain the customs and mores of their homeland while their children are lured by the pattern of the society in which they live. In *Fear Strikes Out*, James Piersall, once known as the bad boy of major league baseball, vividly describes his experience with mental illness. The reader is led to see the influences of Piersall's childhood that perhaps made him incapable of facing the pressures of the adult world, and how the world appears to the mind that is fuzzily succumbing to the pressures. Another story of the unusual life is William O. Douglas' autobiography, *Of Men and Mountains*. Crippled by polio as a child, Douglas undertook mountain climbing as therapy and found it strengthened both his body and spirit, creating a lifelong attachment to the mountain places.

A strange haunting book that is difficult to classify but is a prime favorite with the adolescent reader is *Anne Frank: The Diary of a Young Girl*. Not a novel, it has the qualities of a novel. Anne, a Jewish girl living in Holland, kept a diary of the years that her family were in hiding in the back rooms of a warehouse in Holland during the German occupation in the Second World War. In the context of persecution and war, and knowing Anne Frank's fate, it is a painfully moving record. The Diary is an intimate revelation of an adolescent girl's fumbling efforts to mature through changing relationships with her mother, her father, her sister, a boy, and neighbors. All of this takes place in a kind of test-tube situation of a few rooms with a limited number of people. Anne is desperately baffled by herself. Her story is read sometimes as early as the junior high school years, but in general its greatest impact is with high school girls. In many ways it is the companion piece for *The Catcher in the Rye*, for Anne shows what it is like to be an adolescent girl, as Holden shows what it is like to be an adolescent boy.

Of course, as the adolescent matures, he may want to dip into the classic biographies that are a part of our cultural heritage. No two people would construct exactly the same list of such material, but the number that are both readable and interesting for the adolescent reader is relatively small. Plutarch's *Lives*, in spite of being written by a Greek philosopher in the first to second centuries, is still highly readable in a good translation. Plutarch conceived of presenting forty-six "parallel lives." In each pair he used a Greek and a Roman, comparing and contrasting their experiences, accomplishments, characters. His material was well documented and is the source of much of the information that we have about people of ancient times. Shakespeare, for example, used Plutarch as the source of material for *Julius Caesar*. Even today, Plutarch's biographies are considered models of writing for he presented individuals as real personalities and centered his facts around a unifying idea. One of the best editions for the adolescent reader is Charles Robinson's *Plutarch: Ten Famous Lives*. It follows the standard English translation made by Dryden and Clough but eliminates material that is of interest only to the antiquarian scholar. The ten biographies presented will introduce the teen-ager to some of the better known figures of the ancient world.

Perhaps the most famous biography ever written is James Boswell's *Life of Johnson*. Boswell, a young Scotsman living in the eighteenth century, attached himself to the person he considered the most interesting in his world, Samuel Johnson. He kept minute records, even setting down actual conversations. He liked to manipulate Johnson into a situation so that he could study his reactions. Eventually he wrote down his intensely revealing materials presenting a personal picture of Samuel Johnson which probably rescued the lexicographer from obscurity.

In American literature, Benjamin Franklin's *Autobiography* is perhaps the best known biographical writing. To be sure, Franklin puts his best foot forward as do most people in writing about themselves. Carl van Doren's *Benjamin Franklin* provides a reader with a nice balance, for Van Doren does much to rescue Franklin from the role of paragon of virtue and high thinking and to show him as the brilliant, witty rogue that he was. Lytton Strachey's *Queen Victoria* is one of the landmarks of biographical writing, for it established firmly the biography that attempts to give a centralized picture of a person and his age rather than a detailed account of every incident that happened to the person.

Among the outstanding modern biographies are *The Autobiography of Lincoln Steffens*, Eve Curie's account of her mother, *Madame Curie*, and Carl Sandburg's biographies of Lincoln, *The Prairie Years* and *The War Years*. Several generations of readers have been entertained by Steffens' record of his wealthy childhood and his adult career as a muckraking journalist. Eve Curie's story generates enthusiasm, not only because it deals with a most fascinating personality, but because her mother's marriage bound two people professionally and personally in the pursuit of a scientific truth. Because Miss Curie is an adept and sensitive writer and because of her close relationship to the subject, *Madame Curie* is one of the great biographies. Sandburg, of course, brings to his writing about Lincoln an enthusiastic interest spawned by his own childhood in the Lincoln country of Illinois. He also has great talent in handling language, developed through his writing of poetry. Because Sandburg is basically a poet of the Midwest, he is peculiarly suited to write about Lincoln in his years in pioneer Illinois and creates his picture so that the man and the environment illuminate one another.

It is hard to find the place to stop when talking of biographies. There is Helen Keller's fascinating *Story of My Life* and Winifred Wise's book, *Jane Addams of Hull House.* Still others are Catherine Drinker Bowen's story of Chief Justice Holmes, called *Yankee from Olympus* and Samuel Eliot Morison's, *Christopher Columbus, Mariner.* Morison actually resailed Columbus' voyage in preparation for writing his account of it.

As a person grows up, he comes to know his family, a few friends, and perhaps a teacher or two very well. He may touch the fringes of a number of other people's lives, but only with a small group can he hope to break through the outer shell which we all erect to protect our innermost selves. Biography offers the reader an opportunity to come to know innumerable persons, both living and dead. The reader's life is immeasurably enriched because he can count the great, the daring, the fascinating, among the people that he knows intimately. Their lives touch on his. Such personal knowledge deepens his understandings, both of himself and of his society.

Bibliography

COLLECTED BIOGRAPHY

Beard, Charles A.: *The Presidents in American History*. Messner, 1961; rev. ed., 1965.

Bolton, Sarah K.: *Famous Men of Science*. Crowell, 1946.

Bontemps, Arna: *We Have Tomorrow*. Houghton, 1945.

Boynick, David: *Images of Man*. Prentice, 1963.

Burlingame, Roger: *Scientists Behind the Inventors*. Harcourt, 1960; Avon.

Commager, Henry Steele: *Crusaders for Freedom*. Doubleday, 1962.

De Kruif, Paul: *Microbe Hunters*. Harcourt, 1932; Pocket; Wash. Sq.

Fanning, Leonard M.: *Titans of Business*. Lippincott, 1964.

Gelman, Steve: *Young Olympic Champions*. Norton, 1964.

Hughes, Langston: *Famous American Negroes*, Dodd, 1954.

Jaffe, Bernard: *Men of Science in America*. Simon and Schuster, 1958, rev. ed.

Kennedy, John F.: *Profiles in Courage*. Harper, 1961; Perennial.

Kenworthy, Leonard: *Twelve Citizens of the World*. Doubleday, 1953.

Mantle, Mickey: *The Quality of Courage*. Doubleday, 1965; Bantam.

Poole, Lynn, and Gray Poole: *Scientists Who Changed the World*. Dodd, 1960; Apollo.

Terkel, Studs: *Giants of Jazz*. Crowell, 1957.

Trease, Geoffrey: *Seven Queens of England*. Vanguard, 1953.

————: *Seven Kings of England*. Vanguard, 1955.

Untermeyer, Louis: *Makers of the Modern World*. Simon and Schuster, 1955; Simon and Schuster.

BIOGRAPHIES ESPECIALLY FOR THE ADOLESCENT

Baker, Nina: *Juarez, Hero of Mexico.* Vanguard, 1942.
———: *He Wouldn't Be King: The Story of Simón Bolívar.* Vanguard, 1941.
———: *Garibaldi.* Vanguard, 1944.
———: *Lenin.* Vanguard, 1945.
Baker, Rachel: *First Woman Doctor: The Story of Elizabeth Blackwell, M.D.* Messner, 1944.
Braymer, Marjorie: *The Walls of Windy Troy.* Harcourt, 1960; Voyager.
Daugherty, James: *Abraham Lincoln.* Viking, 1943.
———: *William Blake.* Viking, 1960.
Eaton, Jeanette: *Gandhi, Fighter without a Sword.* Morrow, 1950.
———: *The Story of Eleanor Roosevelt.* Morrow, 1956.
———: *Trumpeter's Tale: The Story of the Young Louis Armstrong.* Morrow, 1955.
Forsee, Alyesa: *Frank Lloyd Wright: Rebel in Concrete.* Macrae, 1959.
Franchere, Ruth: *Jack London: The Pursuit of a Dream.* Crowell, 1962.
Garst, Shannon: *Crazy Horse, Great Warrior of the Sioux.* Houghton, 1950.
———: *James Bowie and His Famous Knife.* Messner, 1955.
———: *Jim Bridger: Greatest of the Mountain Men.* Houghton, 1952.
———: *Kit Carson: Trail Blazer and Scout.* Messner, 1942.
Gibson, Althea: *I Always Wanted to Be Somebody.* Harper, 1958; Perennial.
Gollomb, Joseph: *Albert Schweitzer: Genius of the Jungle.* Vanguard, 1949.
Holt, Rackham: *George Washington Carver: An American Biography.* Doubleday, rev. 1963.
Horgan, Paul: *Citizen of New Salem.* Farrar, Straus, 1961.
Komroff, Manuel: *Mozart.* Knopf, 1956.
———: *Thomas Jefferson.* Messner, 1961.
Kugelmass, J. Alvin: *Ralph J. Bunche: Fighter for Peace.* Messner, rev., 1962.
———: *Roald Amundsen: A Saga of the Polar Seas.* Messner, 1955.
Latham, Jean Lee: *Carry on Mr. Bowditch.* Houghton, 1955.

Levinger, Elma: *Albert Einstein.* Messner, 1949.
Medary, Marjorie: *Each One Teach One: Frank C. Laubach.* McKay, 1954.
Norman, Charles: *To a Different Drum.* Harper, 1954.
Peare, Catherine Owens: *The F.D.R. Story.* Crowell, 1962.
Randall, Ruth Painter: *I, Jessie.* Little, Brown, 1963.
———: *Mary Lincoln: Biography of a Marriage.* Little, Brown, 1953.
Roos, Ann: *Man of Molokai: The Life of Father Damien.* Lippincott, 1943.
Sandburg, Carl: *Abe Lincoln Grows Up.* Harcourt, 1931.
Shippen, Katherine: *Moses.* Harper, 1949.
Waite, Helen Elmira: *How Do I Love Thee? The Story of Elizabeth Barrett Browning.* Macrae, 1953.
Yates, Elizabeth: *Amos Fortune: Free Man.* Dutton, 1950.

PEOPLE WHO HAVE LIVED UNUSUAL LIVES

Anderson, Marian: *My Lord, What a Morning.* Viking, 1956; Avon.
Bannister, Roger: *The Four-Minute Mile.* Dodd, 1955.
Brickhill, Paul: *Reach for the Sky.* Norton, 1954.
Buck, Pearl S.: *My Several Worlds: A Personal Record.* Day, 1954; Pocket.
Clark, Eugenie: *Lady with a Spear.* Harper, 1953; Perennial.
DeMille, Agnes: *Dance to the Piper.* Atlantic–Little, Brown, 1952; Bantam.
Dooley, Thomas A.: *Dr. Tom Dooley: My Story.* Ariel, 1962; New Amer. Lib.
Fermi, Laura: *Atoms in the Family: My Life with Enrico Fermi.* Univ. of Chicago, 1954; Phoenix.
Frank, Anne: *Anne Frank: The Diary of a Young Girl.* Doubleday, 1952; Pocket.
Gunther, John: *Death Be Not Proud.* Harper, 1949; Modern Lib.; Perennial; Pyramid.
Keller, Helen: *The Story of My Life.* Doubleday, 1954; Dell; Airmont.
Malcolm X: *The Autobiography of Malcolm X.* Grove, 1965; Signet.
Mc Fee, John: *A Sense of Where You Are: A Profile of Princeton's Bill Bradley.* Farrar, Straus, 1965; Bantam.
Piersall, Jim, and Albert Hirschberg: *Fear Strikes Out.* Atlantic–Little, Brown, 1955; Bantam.

Washington, Booker T.: *Up from Slavery*. Doubleday, 1901; Bantam.

SAMPLING OF CLASSIC BIOGRAPHY

Boswell, James: *The Life of Samuel Johnson*. Oxford; Scribners; Dell; Mod. Lib. (abridged).

Bowen, Catherine Drinker: *Yankee from Olympus: Justice Holmes and His Family*. Little, Brown, 1944; Bantam.

Chute, Marchette: *Shakespeare of London*. Dutton, 1949; Dutton.

Curie, Eve: *Madame Curie*. Doubleday, 1949; Pocket; Riverside.

Derleth, August: *Concord Rebel: A Life of Henry David Thoreau*. Chilton, 1962; Avon.

Forbes, Esther: *Paul Revere and the World He Lived In*. Houghton, 1962.

Franklin, Benjamin: *Autobiography*. Several editions.

Freeman, Douglas Southall: *Lee of Virginia*. Scribners, 1958.

Ludwig, Emil: *Napoleon*. Mod. Lib.; Tudor; Pocket.

Morison, Samuel Eliot: *Christopher Columbus: Mariner*. Atlantic–Little, Brown, 1955.

Neider, Charles, ed.: *Autobiography of Mark Twain*. Harper, 1959.

Plutarch: *The Lives of the Noble Grecians and Romans*. Mod. Lib.; Selections.

Priestley, J. B.: *Charles Dickens: A Pictorial Biography*. Viking, 1962.

Robinson, Charles A., ed.: *Plutarch: Ten Famous Lives*. Dutton, 1962.

Sandburg, Carl: Vol. I. *Abraham Lincoln: The Prairie Years*. Vol. II. *Abraham Lincoln: The War Years, 1861–1864*. Vol. III. *Abraham Lincoln: The War Years, 1864–1865*. Harcourt, 1954; Dell.

Steffens, Lincoln: *The Autobiography of Lincoln Steffens*. Harcourt, 1936.

Strachey, Lytton: *Queen Victoria*. Harcourt, 1949.

Chapter 12
The Wonderful World of Nonfiction

Every addition to true knowledge is an addition to human power.

Horace Mann

Our children are growing to maturity in a period of exploding knowledge. It is estimated that 90 per cent of all the scientists who have ever lived are alive and working at the present time. Furthermore, no culture has ever been so introspective. As a result, we have great masses of information about all the basic social institutions, about our history, about ourselves. Knowledge is accumulating at such a rate that new theories and "laws" are overturned by more recent discoveries before the man on the street is aware that they exist. It is estimated, for example, that a scientific principle has a life expectancy of about ten years before it will be drastically modified or supplanted by newer information.

So the individual growing up today is faced with a lifelong task of running to catch up. What he learns as fact in school or college will probably not take him more than a few years into his adult life. What he needs in such a world is intellectual curiosity and the techniques through which to satisfy it. He needs to become a "learning" person not a "learned" person.

And most of the resources for learning are available in man's incredible storehouse of books. Not only is human knowledge available in the scholarly and pon-

derous volumes that most of us visualize as the necessary format for such information, but it is available
for the adolescent in works written especially for him,
often profusely illustrated. No people in human history have given more attention to providing a rich
reservoir of factual books for teen-agers than have we
in America in the mid-twentieth century. But unfortunately too few parents are even aware that such
fabulous materials exist, and many teachers working
with adolescents are equally ignorant.

Every year the author reviews approximately a
thousand new books that publishers have brought out
especially for the adolescent reader. Almost two-thirds
of the titles are nonfiction. They are expository accounts of man's work in science, in the social sciences,
in the arts, in technology and business, in hobbies and
leisure activities, and in personal and social problems.
There are books on almost every conceivable subject.
Often times the appeal seems such a limited one that
one wonders if the publisher didn't err in bringing out
the book. For instance, a year or so ago, a book came
out devoted exclusively to the subject of hawks. It
seemed inconceivable that any young person would
want a whole book about hawks. But I heard of a
western Iowa adolescent who had become fascinated
with hawks: had found nestlings, reared them to maturity and taught them to hunt. He was ecstatic to
receive the book because now he could confirm observations he had made and fill in the gaps in his knowledge. The problem is to get the right book to the right
child. Almost without exception there is a useful book
covering any interest that an American teen-ager
might have today.

These books are not so technical that they over-
whelm the young reader. They are not abridged college textbooks, but are written in clear expository
prose. There is a kind of unwritten principle among
educators that might be stated thus: "Whatever is

capable of being explained and understood, can be explained and understood at a simpler level." It is this principle that is exemplified by the nonfiction book for teen-agers. Extremely complicated and difficult developments in human knowledge are presented with clarity and precision. The broad outline sketched is accurate, and the young reader may later refine and add to his knowledge through subsequent study. The discussion that follows centers on certain broad categories of nonfiction.

PERSONAL EXPERIENCE

One type of very appealing nonfiction book is the account of a vivid experience that an individual has undergone, most often one that is quite out of the ordinary. Through such accounts, the reader may find out what life is like in remote parts of the world. With De Poncins he can live a year with the Eskimos in the northern part of Canada by reading the book *Kabloona*. He may find out something about the customs and ways of life of Mexican families through *My Heart Lies South*, the story of an American girl who falls in love and marries a Mexican from a wealthy family. Van der Post in *A View of All the Russias* tells of his trip through Russia as a tourist, his talks with people in restaurants and on the streets and trains, his encounters with officialdom, his observations of Russian cultural activities and daily life. In *Journey Behind the Iron Curtain*, Westbrook, an American high school student, writes of his observations of Russia while on a summer trip with fellow classmates. It is a personal account of the young man's reactions to his experiences. Or there is the charming book, *Persia Revisited*. Told by an American woman, Mrs. Mehdevi, who is married to a Persian, it describes the couple's return to her husband's ancestral home after years of living in the West. *Reveille for a Persian Vil-*

lage is written by a Persian woman who trains as a sociologist and then goes to one of the small villages of her country to try and find a way of helping her people help themselves. Santha Rama Rau's *Home to India* is the recounting of the experiences of a daughter of an Indian ambassador, reared in the capitals of the world, who returns to her own native culture. She sees Indian life both as an insider and as a stranger to it. *Eighth Moon* is one of the few pictures of life in Red China today. Sansan Lord, the author, was the daughter of a Chinese foreign diplomat. She was separated from her parents at the time of the Communist revolution and had grown up in China until her parents were able to arrange for her crossing the border into Hong Kong. Her account of life as a schoolgirl and adolescent in Communist China is a vivid one with no tinge of vindictiveness.

Sometimes it is refreshing to see one's own country afresh. A book like John Steinbeck's *Travels with Charley* is a delightful tale of the author's trip, taken with an elderly poodle in a truck trailer, across the United States. In his travels Steinbeck rediscovers the people, their traditions, the landscape.

The personal experience story, besides giving the reader a feeling for different parts of the world, may also allow him to share in some of the great adventures and feats of physical endurance on the last frontiers of our world. *Endurance*, by Alfred Lansing, tells of Shackleton's incredible journey in the Antarctic when his ship sank and he and his men were forced to pitch camp on a drifting ice floe. The men survived the almost impossible task of crossing one of the most storm-torn oceans on the globe in open boats and of hiking across the mountains of South Georgia. In *Annapurna*, Maurice Herzog tells of the magnificent ordeal of a group of French mountain-climbers as they strive to scale one of the towering peaks in the Himalayas. Michel Siffre describes in *Beyond Time* his

sixty-three days spent in the bowels of the earth. There
in the darkness and solitude of a cave he tried to find
out what happens to human beings who are cut off
from the usual elements of light, sound, and compan-
ionship. *Kon-Tiki*, written by a Danish anthropologist,
Thor Heyerdahl, is a classic report of the group of
scientists who constructed a balsa raft according to
the models of the ancient Incas and then set sail across
the Pacific toward the Polynesian islands. They were
attempting to prove that such a journey might have
been possible for the ancient people. Through this
kind of book the reader can share in the feats of exploration and daring of man investigating his world.

There is also a documentary type of personal experience in which the writer attempts to explore the
inner workings of the mind of a person involved in
a particular experience. He may probe the psychology
of the criminal, the dope addict, the alcoholic. He
may describe the life of the religious recluse or the
heroism of John F. Kennedy when his PT boat was
wrecked. Or he may show the strange relationship
that can develop between man and beast as in *Born
Free* and *Living Free*, by Joy Adamson, or *All Creatures, Great and Small*, by Daniel Mannix. Jim Bishop
attempts to recreate moment by moment a particular
time in history in his books *The Day Christ Was Born*,
The Day Lincoln Was Shot or *A Day in the Life of
President Kennedy*. In *Collision Course*, a boy can
become involved with the crew during the last hours
of the *Andrea Doria* before she sank; in *With All My
Love* a girl will be affected by the experiences of
Penny DeFore, an actor's daughter who went to Korea
to work in an orphanage set up for war victims. Such
documentary accounts of personal experience give the
reader the opportunity to share extraordinary moments
and to come to an understanding about the level of
achievement that man can reach under trying circumstances.

ARCHAEOLOGY AND ANTHROPOLOGY

In the last few years there have been many books presenting the work of archaeologists and anthropologists to adolescents. It has been pointed out that the further man moves from his origins, the more he knows about them. The two fields devoted to the study of man and the development of his culture are rather recent additions to scientific research. Interest in the remnants of past civilizations did not develop until a hundred years ago, and the study of the origins of man is an outgrowth of Darwin's theory of evolution postulated in 1859. Friedman's *Man in the Making* is a readable story of the work of anthropologists as they attempt to build a picture of man and his life in prehistoric times. Leonard Cottrell's *Lost Cities* is an excellent account of the discovery of a series of ruins of ancient cities located on different continents of the world. The chapters read like mystery stories starting with the legends, moving on to the long search, and ending with the eventual discovery, which is often accidental. The book also presents what is known or surmised about the people who built and occupied these magnificent cities. Shirley Gorenstein has written an exciting book called *Introduction to Archaeology* which describes how archaeologists work, and incidentally gives a number of romantic touches that accompany the profession. Von Hagen's books about the Incas and the Aztecs are some of the best accounts we have of these two great civilizations that existed in the New World at the time of their European discovery. Twenty-five years ago this type of book was almost nonexistent for the adolescent reader. Now each year four or five exciting new narratives about the discoveries recently made of man's great past are published.

SOCIAL SCIENCES

In the broad area of the social sciences are books designed for the adolescent reader that cover every conceivable aspect of man's long struggle to find techniques of living together in groups. One of the books that provides an excellent introduction to the social sciences is *The Sciences of Mankind*. In this book Jane Watson has described the variety of work performed by social scientists in the field of human relationships.

A number of fascinating books deal with the differing cultures of the world. For example, there is the Land and People Series. These are fairly short, profusely illustrated accounts of individual countries. They include a short history, an overview of the geography, and material on the culture, the government, and the economy of the country. In addition to such a series, there are many individual volumes. Two relatively new books are *The Japanese*, by Robert Newman, and *Israel Reborn*, by Oden Meeker, both of which contain accurate facts essential for the vivid depiction of each country.

Another kind of social studies book is the one explaining something about the workings of our own governmental institutions. There are a whole series of these. Gerald Johnson has written three: *The Presidency, The Congress,* and *The Supreme Court*. These give the history and development of each institution and good clear information about its current status and operation. *Your Magnificent Declaration*, by Bruce and E. B. Findlay, is an exciting book on the Declaration of Independence and its current significance. *Your Freedoms: The Bill of Rights*, by Frank Kelly, takes up the first ten amendments to the constitution and shows our continuing struggle to define them in terms of the changing conditions of our lives. *Obsta-*

cle Course on Capitol Hill vividly presents our Congress in action. The book gives a lively picture of a new congressman breaking into his new job, and through his experiences details the step-by-step procedures from the initiation of a bill to its arrival on the floor of Congress.

There are also books suitable for the teen-ager concerned with the current social problems of our period. *The Automation Age,* by Pauline Arnold and Percival White, details the steady movement toward an automated society and poses the problem of what cybernetics means to human society. Rachel Carson's exposé of the misuses of insecticides in *The Silent Spring* is a terrifying disclosure of the use of poisons. In *The Fire Next Time,* James Baldwin sharply draws the picture of the embittered Negro in American society. Claude Brown's *Manchild in the Promised Land* also describes the life of the Negro shackled by convention. There are many books about Communism especially geared to the young reader. David Footman's book, *The Russian Revolutions,* gives an excellent presentation of the conditions and the movements that led up to the 1917 revolution when the Czars were overthrown and the dictatorship of the proletariat established.

Stocks and Bonds, by Donald and Rose Sobol, is highly readable and gives a clear picture of the nature of stocks and bonds and how they function in the financial world. This particular title is a sample of the kind of specialized volume that one can find to meet almost any kind of interest a teen-ager may have.

In addition, there are many historical books, often specialized. *Guns of the Old West* describes and illustrates the weapons that opened up the West, and tells the stories of the men who used them. Walter Webb's *The Great Plains* and Floyd Streeter's *Prairie Trails and Cow Towns* are two of the studies of the American West. There are works dealing with daily life in ancient Rome, during the Renaissance in Europe, and during the Puritan Reformation in England.

The future also is the subject of some informational books. *Keeping Ahead of Machines*, by Cornelia Spencer, and *You and the Next Decade*, by Adrian A. Paradis, are both excellent books which speculate about the kinds of changes that may take place in society because of the increased use of machines. D. S. Halacy's *Nine Roads to Tomorrow* is a survey of breakthroughs in the use of laser, Comsat, and bionics.

SCIENTIFIC BOOKS

There are beautifully illustrated, accurately and clearly written books for teen-agers about almost every aspect of scientific development. The works are attractively bound and are often beautiful examples of the printer's art. Any adolescent who wants technical, scientific information, often far in advance of his science courses, can have it at his fingertips.

In astronomy, two relatively new books are Ben Bova's *The Milky Way Galaxy* and *Pictorial Astronomy*, by Alter, Cleminshaw, and Phillips. Representative of the wealth of exciting books in physics is *Inside the Nucleus*, by Irving Adler, which reports the development of nuclear physics step by step in such a way that anyone can understand it. *Masers and Lasers*, by H. Arthur Klein, is a whole book devoted to the amazing uses of light rays. His descriptions provide a virtual survey of modern physics. George Gamow's *A Planet Called Earth* is an intriguing account of earth science, while Louis Wolfe's *Probing the Atmosphere* traces the long history of meteorology from the days of the cave man to present-day knowledge to future possibilities.

Psychology and human biology are explored in many books. McBain and Johnson in *The Science of Ourselves* present elementary psychological concepts and include a number of suggested experiments. Margaret Hyde's *Your Brain: Master Computer* is perhaps the best presentation of what is now known about the operation of the mind. And a particularly good book about human life is Huff and Kovarsky's *Cycles in Your Life*. Here the authors discuss the whole concept of cycles: cycles in nature, in history, in economics, in fashion, in astronomy. Then they demonstrate the apparent importance of such cyclic organization to satisfactory human living.

Biology is also represented by such books as *You and Your Cells*, by Leo Schneider, who has written a precise and clear explanation of the cellular constitution of living tissue. The mysterious DNA is clearly and carefully explained by Edward Frankel in *DNA— Ladder of Life*. *From Cell to Test Tube*, by Chambers and Payne, is an introduction to biochemistry, describing not only certain basic research studies but also some possible applications. A more mature but still eminently readable book is *The New Intelligent Man's Guide to Science*, by Isaac Asimov. The author, himself a scientist and a prolific writer, gives in this volume a kind of summing up of "what every man" should know and needs to know in each of the basic areas of science.

MATHEMATICS

Every year a handful of books appear that capture within their covers the romance of mathematics. Sometimes these are books of "puzzlers" that the student must try to solve for himself. More often they take him into the exciting history of mathematics. For example, Leon Terry's *The Mathmen* allocates a chapter to each of the great ancient Greek mathematicians and their discoveries. Constance Reid's *A Long Way from Euclid* is a history of mathematics which comes down to such modern concepts as topology and symbolic logic. The theory and story of computers are unfolded by Vorwald and Clark in a book entitled *Computers.*

COMMUNICATIONS

A whole array of books deals with the systems that man has slowly and painfully developed to help him shape the world of nature to his own ends and understanding. These are often systems so familiar to the average person that we do not think about them at all. But each is a fascinating story. Neal's *Communication: From Stone Age to Space Age* traces the development of communication systems from cave drawings and sign language to printing and television. Brown's *Map Making: The Art that Became a Science* deals with man's long, long struggle to map his world accurately. The book is illustrated profusely with examples of early maps. In *The Romance of Weights and Measures,* Keith Gordon Irwin traces the story of man's fumbling attempts to work out a way of measuring and weighing. *The Treasure of Our Tongue,* by Barnett, is a good introductory book for the adolescent on the origin and evolution of the English language.

FINE ARTS

Books in the fine arts are beautifully printed and richly illustrated. *The Story of Design,* by Marion Downer, is a handsome book that traces great art and craft work from its beginnings in prehistoric times down to the present. In the area of painting there are many possible introductory books. Thomas Craven's large *Rainbow Book of Art* has been used in high school libraries to give an overview of great painting. *The Visual Experience,* by Bates Lowry, treats the same subject but is for a somewhat more sophisticated reader. A fairly extensive text accompanies the illustrations and discusses what one looks at and for in a work of art.

In music, Shippen and Seidlova's *The Heritage of Music* is a good beginning point for the novice. A complementary book is Elie Siegmeister's *Invitation to Music*, designed to increase both understanding and appreciation of various forms and types of music rather than to present its historical development. One of the most interesting books for many adolescents is *What Jazz Is All About*, by Lillian Erlich. The author's account of the growth of jazz includes biographical sketches of the great jazz artists and attempts to explain what directions contemporary jazz is taking and why.

Eyes on the Ballet, by Katherine Sorley Walker, gives a sound, over-all picture of the classic dance. Although it does contain a short history, the major part of the book is about the great artists and the exciting movements in the field today. *American Modern Dancers*, by Olga Maynard, is one of the best books to give the adolescent information about the rise of the modern dance, a unique American form.

Paul Engle has edited a volume *On Creative Writing*. This book grew out of his long and successful experience in directing the writers' workshop at the University of Iowa. Each chapter is written by a practicing writer who describes the problems inherent in writing each of the various literary genres: the short story, the poem, the popular article, the novel. The discussion is followed by a sample of the literary type which demonstrates the points made in the discussion.

Books narrating personal experiences, books centering on historical events, books about science and math, books about the art forms, books on literature and writing—these are only some of the wealth of nonfiction available to American adolescents. Such works help a young person gain a vision of the world and

of man's knowledge. No longer is the child blocked
off from information because there is no material available that he can comprehend. It is there. The most
complicated concepts that man has developed are now
explained in language that a young person can grasp.
The problem that has evolved from this great mass of
published nonfiction is one of logistics: how can the
adolescent who wants information on a specialized
subject find just the right book? To help solve this
dilemma, you should become aware of your son's or
daughter's interests and curiosities. It is all too easy
to turn aside each flickering spark of interest and kill
intellectual curiosity with the excuse that the right
book is not at hand. Encourage your questioning teen-
ager to go to a library. Better still, make the trip with
him. If the right book is not available, go with the
youngster to a book store. You will both enjoy browsing for a half an hour, and you will see how one book
usually leads to another.

Bibliography

PERSONAL EXPERIENCE

Adamson, Joy: *The Story of Elsa.* Harcourt Brace, 1965.
    Strange relationship that develops between the author and
    a lioness she adopts as a cub in Kenya.
Bishop, Jim: *The Day Christ Died.* Harper, 1957; Perennial.
    An imaginary moment-by-moment account of the day of
    the crucifixion.
————: *The Day Christ Was Born.* Harper, 1957; Pocket. A
    similarly detailed account of the Nativity.
————: *The Day Lincoln Was Shot.* Harper, 1955; Perennial.
    Using historical details, the author recreates, minute by
    minute, Lincoln's assassination and death.
Brodkorb, Reider: *Flying Free.* Rand McNally, 1965. A Nor-
    wegian tells of his passion for eagles from boyhood to
    adult life.

DeFore, Penny: *With All My Love*. Prentice, 1965. The daughter of a movie actor goes to Korea to serve in an orphanage.

Donovan, Robert: *PT-109: John F. Kennedy in World War II*. A re-creation of Kennedy's experiences as commander of a PT boat which was sunk, stranding its crew on a small island in the Pacific.

Herzog, Maurice: *Annapurna*. Dutton, 1953; Pocket. A detailed account of the scaling of a Himalayan peak by a French expedition.

Heyerdahl, Thor: *Kon-Tiki*. Rand McNally, 1950; Pocket; Rand McNally; Wash. Sq. A Danish anthropologist constructs a balsa raft and sails it with a crew of five to the South Pacific islands.

Keith, Agnes Newton: *Three Came Home*. Little, Brown, 1947; Macfadden. Experiences of the author in a prisoner of war camp in the South Pacific during the Second World War.

Lansing, Alfred: *Endurance*. McGraw, 1959; Avon. The story of Shackleton's remarkable feat in sailing 800 miles in a whaling boat to South Georgia and making the first crossing of that island in order to lead rescue groups to his men stranded on Elephant Island.

Lord, Sansan, and Bette Lord: *Eighth Moon*. Harper, 1965. The daughter of a Chinese diplomat grows to maturity in Red China until rescued by her expatriate family.

Lord, Walter: *A Night to Remember*. Holt, 1955; Bantam. The story of the sinking of the *Titanic*.

————: *A Time to Stand*. Harper, 1961; Pocket. A reconstruction of the Battle of the Alamo.

Mannix, Daniel P.: *All Creatures, Great and Small*. McGraw, 1963. A naturalist tells his enchanting experiences with a variety of animals.

Mehdevi, Anne Sinclair: *Persia Revisited*. Knopf, 1964. The American wife of a Persian aristocrat finds adjustment to her husband's home and family often difficult.

Monat, Pawel, and John Dille: *Spy in the U.S.* Harper, 1962; Berkley. A former enemy spy assigned to the United States tells of his espionage activities in our country.

Moscow, Alvin: *Collision Course*. Putnam, 1959. A detailed account of the sinking of the *Andrea Dorea*.

Najafi, Najmeh, and Helen Hinckley: *Reveille for a Persian Village*. Harper, 1958. A Persian woman, trained as a sociologist, tells of her experiences in working with a small provincial village in her own country.

Rama Rau, Santha: *Home to India*. Harper, 1945; Perennial.

182 NONFICTION

The experiences of an adolescent reared in the West when
she returns to her aristocratic Indian family.
Sayre, Woodrow W.: *Four Against Everest*. Prentice, 1964.
A nonprofessional group makes an assault on Everest.
Siffre, Michel: *Beyond Time*. McGraw, 1964. The author
spends three months in a French cave to study the psychological effects of such dislocation.
Steinbeck, John: *Travels with Charley*. Viking, 1962; Bantam.
Steinbeck and his poodle, Charley, make a sentimental
journey across America, reacting to the landscape and its
people.
Treviño, Elizabeth B.: *My Heart Lies South*. Crowell, 1953.
An American woman's experiences in marrying into a
wealthy Mexican family.
Van der Loeff, A. Rutgers, and Anna Basenau: *Avalanche*. Morrow, 1958. The dramatic account of an avalanche that
swept away a Swiss village.
Westbrook, Robert: *Journey Behind the Iron Curtain*. Putnam,
1963. A teen-age boy's account of his summer trip to
Russia.

ARCHAEOLOGY AND ANTHROPOLOGY

Cottrell, Leonard: *Digs and Diggers*. World, 1964. The story
of archaeology is told through discoveries made of prehistoric man, in Egypt, the Far East, and the New World.
————: *Land of the Pharaohs*. World Pub., 1960. Discovery
of King Tut's tomb serves as a springboard for a description of the living conditions of ancient Egypt.
————: *Lost Cities*. Holt, 1957; Universal Lib., 1963. Account
of discovery of the ruins of thirteen once-great cities.
Falls, C. B.: *The First 3000 Years*. Viking, 1960. An account
of the beginnings of civilization.
Friedman, Estelle: *Man in the Making*. Putnam, 1960. The
work of anthropologists as they build a picture of man and
his life in prehistoric times.
Glubok, Shirley: *The Fall of the Aztecs*. St. Martin's, 1965. The
story of Cortez' conquest of the Aztecs, told through the
diary of a Spanish soldier and illustrated with drawings
made by an Indian witness.
Gorenstein, Shirley: *Introduction to Archaeology*. Basic Books,
1965. Describes how archaeologists work.

Irwin, Constance: *Fair Gods and Stone Faces.* St. Martin's, 1963. A book of archaeological detective work which attempts to prove that the great civilizations of America's past are linked to that of the ancient Mediterranean world.

Heyerdahl, Thor: *Aku Aku.* Rand McNally, 1958. A study of the civilizations of the Easter Islands, which attempts to find the origins of the great stone heads facing the sea.

Lissner, Ivar: *The Silent Past.* Putnam, 1962; Pocket. From small bits of information the author reconstructs cultures of the world that have left almost no trace.

Marriott, Alice L.: *The First Comers.* McKay, 1960. Fairly comprehensive picture of what is known of the early American Indians.

Samachson, Dorothy, and Joseph Samachson: *Good Digging.* Rand McNally, 1960; Rand McNally. Narrates a series of famous archaeological expeditions and what they uncovered.

Sanderson, I. T.: *The Monkey Kingdom.* Chilton, 1963. Definitive information about the primates shows many of the roots of human behavior present in animal patterns.

Silverberg, Robert: *Lost Cities and Vanished Civilizations.* Chilton, 1962; Bantam. The stories of six great ancient civilizations uncovered at Pompeii, Troy, Knossos, and elsewhere.

Von Hagen, Victor W.: *Incas, People of the Sun.* World Pub., 1961. Describes the culture of the Incas of ancient Peru.

————: *Sun Kingdom of the Aztecs.* World Pub., 1958. Discusses what is known of the Aztec civilization of Mexico.

SOCIAL SCIENCES

Arnold, Pauline, and Percival White: *The Automation Age.* Holiday, 1960. Pictures the development of automation and its influence on our social life.

Baldwin, James: *The Fire Next Time.* Dial, 1963; Dell; Delta. Letters by Baldwin to his nephew. They create both understanding and apprehension of the Negro's situation.

Bendiner, Robert: *Obstacle Course on Capitol Hill.* McGraw, 1964. The way that Congress works, illustrated by the experiences of a young Congressman breaking into his new job.

Berger, Josef, and Lawrence C. Wroth: *Discoverers of the New*

World. Harper, 1960. Deals with the three centuries of discovery and exploration between the fifteenth and eighteenth centuries.

Brooks, Polly S., and Nancy Walworth: *The World Awakes.* Lippincott, 1962. Using biographical sketches, the book presents the meaning of the Renaissance in Italy, Spain, France, and England.

Brumberg, Abraham, and Richard M. Ketchum, eds.: *What Is Communism?* Rev. ed. Dutton. An account of the principles of Communism in theory and practice, told from a Western point of view.

Buckmaster, Henrietta: *Flight to Freedom.* Crowell, 1958. The story of the underground railroads during the Civil War.

Carr, Donald E.: *The Breath of Life.* Norton, 1965. The problem of air pollution is explored.

Cavanah, Frances, and Elizabeth Crandall: *Meet the Presidents.* Macrae, 1964. Brief sketches of each of the Presidents with selection of colorful and humanizing details about each.

Findlay, Bruce A., and E. B. Findlay: *Your Magnificent Declaration.* Holt, 1962. The history, meaning, and importance of the Declaration of Independence.

Footman, David: *The Russian Revolutions.* Putnam, 1964. Traces the history of Russia's revolt against its rulers during the early years of the twentieth century.

Foster, Genevieve: *The World of Columbus and Sons.* Scribners, 1965. A "horizontal" picture of history traces what was happening throughout the world at the time of Columbus.

Gaer, Joseph: *What the Great Religions Believe.* Dodd, 1963, Signet. Defines religion and gives a short explanation of the basic tenets of the major religions of the world.

Halacy, D. S., Jr.: *Nine Roads to Tomorrow.* Macrae, 1964. Breakthroughs on scientific and technological fronts that stagger the imagination with their possibilities.

Harrison, C. William: *Conservation: The Challenge of Reclaiming Our Plundered Land.* Messner, 1963. Discussion of the plundering of the natural resources of the American continent.

Johnson, Gerald W.: *The Congress.* Morrow, 1963. Here is the whole process of Congress: how a bill is introduced, how committees work, the struggle for power and the dangers of investigations.

————: *The Presidency.* Morrow, 1962. Presents the importance of the President of the United States and traces his changing role through our history.

————: *The Supreme Court*. Morrow, 1962. The history of the Supreme Court and its impact on American democracy.

Kelly, Frank K.: *Your Freedoms: The Bill of Rights*. Putnam, 1964. Lucid discussion of the first 10 amendments to the Constitution presenting the continuing struggle to interpret them in a changing world.

Lavender, David: *Westward Vision: The Story of the Oregon Trail*. McGraw, 1963. An accurate account of the development and the history of the Oregon Trail.

Lens, Sidney: *Working Men: The Story of Labor*. Putnam, 1960. The history of the rise of American labor unions.

McCart, Samuel W.: *Trial By Jury: A Complete Guide to the Jury System*. Chilton, 1964. Traces the historical development of the jury system and examines its status in our society today.

Meeker, Oden: *Israel Reborn*. Scribners, 1963. The story of the development of modern Israel.

Newman, Robert: *The Japanese: People of the Three Treasures*. Atheneum, 1964. Brief survey of the political, cultural, and social history of the Japanese.

Paradis, Adrian A.: *You and the Next Decade*. McKay, 1964. Problems the individual faces in today's world because of increasing mechanization and new economic conditions.

Richards, Leverett G.: *Ice Age Coming?* Day, 1960. The most recent information about the cause of the ice ages of the past leads to speculations about their recurrence in the future.

Sobol, Donald, and Rose Sobol: *Stocks and Bonds*. Watts, 1963. Guide to the financial world of stocks and bonds: what they are, why and how companies issue them, and why and how investors buy them.

Spencer, Cornelia: *Keeping Ahead of Machines*. Day, 1965. Crucial social and personal problems of the modern world resulting from cybernetics.

Streeter, Floyd B.: *Prairie Trails and Cow Towns*. Devin, 1963. The "classic" treatment of the early trails and towns of the West.

Watson, Jane W.: *The Sciences of Mankind*. Golden Press, 1960. Presents the work of the social scientists in their diverse fields and their contributions to the understanding of man.

Webb, Walter P.: *The Great Plains*. Grossett, 1957; Universal

Library. The authoritative treatment of the history of the plains and their profound impact on America's development.

Whitehead, Don: *Border Guard: The Story of the U.S. Customs Service.* Avon, 1964 (S144); McGraw, 1963. The U.S. Customs Service's war against dope and smugglers is told through many actual incidents.

SCIENCE

Adler, Irving: *Inside the Nucleus.* Day, 1963; Signet. The development of nuclear physics for the uninformed reader.

Allen, Thomas B.: *The Quest.* Chilton, 1965. Facts about the search for extraterrestrial life.

Alter, Dinsmore, and others: *Pictorial Astronomy.* 2nd Rev. Crowell, 1963. Profusely illustrated introduction to astronomy and the wonders of the heavens.

Asimov, Isaac: *The New Intelligent Man's Guide to Science.* Basic Books, 1965. Almost a desk reference to basic information in the modern sciences.

Bova, Ben: *The Milky Way Galaxy: Man's Exploration of the Stars.* Holt, 1961. Up-to-date synopsis of knowledge about the nature of the Milky Way.

Chambers, Robert W., and Alma Payne: *From Cell to Test Tube.* Scribners, 1960; Scribners. Introduction to biochemistry describing experiments and applications.

Cline, Barbara Lovett: *The Questioners: Physicists and the Quantum Theory.* Crowell, 1965. Chapter accounts of the struggle of physicists, particularly those working on the quantum theory.

Dickinson, Alice: *Charles Darwin and Natural Selection.* Watts, 1964. Emphasizes not only the life of Darwin but also the revolutionary nature of his theories and how he arrived at them.

Disraeli, Robert: *New Worlds Through the Microscope.* Viking, 1960. Descriptions of the "invisible" world with excellent examples of microphotography.

Dunsheath, Percy: *Electricity: How It Works.* Crowell, 1960. Historical account of the wonders of electricity.

Frankel, Edward: *DNA—Ladder of Life.* McGraw, 1964. Clear, nontechnical presentation of DNA, the mysterious program tapes within cells.

Gamow, George: *A Planet Called Earth*. Viking, 1963; Bantam. An excellent presentation of earth science.

Gaskell, Thomas F., and Thomas Frohock: *The World Beneath the Oceans*. Doubleday, 1964. Discusses the science of oceanography.

Gramet, Charles: *Reproduction and Sex in Animal Life*. Abelard, 1962. Straightforward, simply presented information about the process of reproduction from one-celled animals to man.

Huff, Darrell, and Anatol Kovarsky: *Cycles in Your Life*. Norton, 1964. Deals with all kinds of cycles operating in life, from the cycle of seasons to cycles in moods.

Hyde, Margaret O.: *Your Brain: Master Computer*. McGraw, 1964. An account of what is known about the brain and how it works.

Klein, H. Arthur: *Masers and Lasers*. Lippincott, 1963. The discovery and amazing uses of light rays offer a good introduction to modern physics.

McBain, William M., and R. C. Johnson: *The Science of Ourselves*. Harper, 1962. Introduction to human psychology with many simple experiments for the reader to perform to find out about himself.

Martin, Lealon: *The Conquest of Disease*. Coward, 1961. Achievements in detection, prevention, and control of diseases.

Noshpitz, Joseph: *Understanding Ourselves: The Challenge of the Human Mind*. Coward, 1964. Deals with what psychology has to offer in helping a person understand himself.

Schneider, Leo: *You and Your Cells*. Harcourt, 1964. Introductory but detailed description of what is known of cellular structure.

Wolfe, Louis: *Probing the Atmosphere*. Putnam, 1961. Traces the development of the science of meteorology from the cave man to speculations about future control of the weather.

MATHEMATICS

Barr, Stephen: *Experiments in Topology*. Crowell, 1964. Presents the new area of math, topology.

DeLacy, Estelle: *Euclid and Geometry*. Watts, 1963. The history of geometry starting with Euclid.

Diggins, Julia E.: *String, Straightedge and Shadow.* Viking, 1965, The story of geometry.

Reid, Constance: *A Long Way From Euclid.* Crowell, 1963. The history of mathematics from the Greeks down to topology and symbolic logic.

Terry, Leon: *The Mathmen.* McGraw, 1964. Individual chapters deal with the great, ancient Greek mathematicians and their discoveries.

Vorwald, Alan, and F. Clark: *Computers.* McGraw, 1964. A clear explanation of the basic theory and working of modern computers.

COMMUNICATIONS

Asimov, Isaac: *Words from the Myths.* Houghton, 1961. Through a retelling of the Greek myths, the roots of hundreds of words in the English language are uncovered.

Barnett, Lincoln K.: *The Treasure of Our Tongue.* Knopf, 1965. The history of the English language.

Burgess, Anthony: *Language Made Plain.* Crowell, 1965. Good clear explanation of the nature of language and how it develops.

Coombs, Charles: *Window on the World.* World Pub., 1965. Detailed explanation of the workings of television.

Foster, G. Allen: *Communication: From Primitive Tom-toms to Telstar.* Criterion, 1965. History of communication from the origin of language to Telstar.

Huxley, Julian, and Ludwig Koch: *Animal Language.* Grosset, 1964. Discusses the attempts of modern scientists to record, classify, and decode animal sounds.

Irwin, Keith Gordon: *The Romance of Weights and Measures.* Viking, 1960. Traces man's struggle to find a system for weighing and measuring and its impact on international life.

————: *The 365 Days.* Crowell, 1963. An account giving the history of the calendar.

Laffin, John: *Codes and Ciphers.* Abelard, 1964. All kinds of codes that have been used from earliest times are discussed with many codes given that students can use.

Lambert, Eloise, and Mario Pei: *Our Names: Where They Came From and What They Mean.* Lothrop, 1960. The origin and meanings of hundreds of common names are given.

Neal, Harry E.: *Communication: From Stone Age to Space Age.*
Messner, 1960. History of man's communication efforts
from the cave drawings and sign language to television.

FINE ARTS

Baker, Samm S.: *Your Key to Creative Thinking.* Harper, 1962;
Bantam. Discussion of the nature of creativity with a
series of puzzle exercises to test and evaluate one's own
creative power.

Chute, Marchette: *Stories from Shakespeare.* World Pub., 1956;
Mentor (MT257); New Amer. Lib. Delightful synopses of
Shakespeare's plays told by a leading Shakespearean
scholar.

Country Beautiful Editors: *The Beauty of America in Great
American Art.* Morrow. The American landscape and
people as portrayed by American artists.

Craven, Thomas: *The Rainbow Book of Art.* World Pub., 1956.
Highly successful collection of great masterpieces to be
used to develop familiarity with them.

Downer, Marion: *The Story of Design.* Lothrop, 1963. Great
art and craft work is organized and discussed in a historical pattern reaching back to prehistoric times.

Engle, Paul: *On Creative Writing.* Dutton, 1964. Excellent
discussions of each of the major literary forms by persons
who excel in the areas.

Erlich, Lillian: *What Jazz Is All About.* Messner, 1962. A history of jazz with sketches of great artists of jazz and
what they are attempting to do.

Gettings, Fred: *The Meaning and Wonder of Art.* Golden
Press, 1964. Depicts art as a wonderful adventure that
makes life more meaningful and exciting.

Jones, LeRoi: *Blues People: Negro Music in White America.*
Morrow, 1963; Apollo. The story of jazz becomes also the
story of the Negro's struggle for equal rights.

Lowry, Bates: *The Visual Experience.* Abrams, 1960. A book
on how to appreciate art by detailed analyses of what one
looks for in painting.

Maynard, Olga: *American Modern Dancers.* Little, Brown,
1965; Mentor. A discussion of the rise and meaning of the
modern dance.

Randolph, David: *This Is Music.* McGraw, 1964. Nontechnical

explanation of musical forms and content with emphasis
on musical appreciation.

Rogers, William G.: *A Picture Is a Picture*. Harcourt, 1964 An
examination of modern painting and what it is attempting.

Shippen, Katherine B., and Anca Seidlova: *The Heritage of
Music*. Viking, 1963. History of music from the ancient
Greeks to contemporaries.

Siegmeister, Elie: *Invitation to Music*. Harvey, 1961. Shows
how to understand and appreciate various forms and types
of music.

Walker, Katherine S.: *Eyes on the Ballet*. Day, 1965. Good discussion of the meaning and glory of ballet.

Chapter 13
Reading for the College Bound

Education is a controlling grace to the young, consolation
to the old, wealth to the poor, and ornament to the rich.
Diogenes

We Americans believe deeply in the goodness of education. We were the first people on earth to set up a common school free of charge for all young people regardless of their native abilities. And it naturally follows that believing some education to be good we think more education is better. So our public school system now includes colleges and universities, for we feel that it is the right of everyone to have a chance for a college education.

Though many of the young people graduating from high school will immediately go to work, attend a specialized school for vocational training, or become housewives, millions are going on to college. Colleges are overwhelmed by the number of applicants and have become increasingly selective. Obviously it is a waste of money and effort for a college to attempt to work with students who lack the ability or the preparation or the interest that are necessary for success in the programs offered.

If your child is in the last years of high school, you should realistically appraise his chances of success in college. Discuss the matter with his teachers, the school guidance counselor, and with your youngster. Consider the following questions:

1. Are the child's grades largely A's and B's in his

high school courses? Of course, he may slip in an occasional subject. In fact he may even fail one. Because there is a tendency for college grades to be about a grade point lower than high school grades, a majority of *C* and *D* grades on his high school record indicates that the student is a risk.

2. *Does he stand at the 75th percentile or better on most parts of a standardized achievement test?* Most good high schools today use some sort of national achievement test. These tests are divided into a number of sections covering the academic skills developed in a good educational program. Through such test scores you can compare your son or daughter with young people of the same age throughout the country. The 75th percentile means that an individual is better than 75 per cent of people of similar age and not as good as 25 per cent in his performance of this particular skill.

3. *Does your child read adult material for general comprehension at a speed of 300 to 500 words per minute?* Speed is obviously not so important as comprehension, but it is an external factor that correlates highly with comprehension. An adolescent can test himself by choosing an article in a magazine like *Harper's*, estimating the number of words it contains, and then timing himself to see how long it takes to read it. You can estimate his comprehension by asking him to summarize the article orally for you.

4. *Can he write a 500-word paper that is logically organized and relatively free from gross errors in spelling, punctuation, and grammar?* Read a paper he has prepared. Does the language flow smoothly? Do the ideas follow one another logically? Does his writing seem relatively free of spelling and grammatical errors? If he is having trouble with his writing in high school, he may have problems not only in freshman composition classes but in any college class that requires a lengthy written report.

If you can give an affirmative answer to three out of the four questions above, your son or daughter will probably be successful in college. But your adolescent needs more than an ability to perform certain skills. His success may also depend on what he has read in these preparatory years and on his attitudes toward reading. Too often a young person is a senior in high school before he realizes the great gaps in his reading background. A crash program of reading at this time is seldom effective, for background materials are accumulated slowly and continuously from preschool days.

A body of literature that we might designate a "cultural reservoir" is valuable for any child whether he eventually becomes a chemist, a plumber, a contractor, a lawyer, a teacher, a truck driver, or a doctor. With the knowledge he gains from such literature, a young person knows the meaning of *Gemini*, as the name of a spaceship, or *Titan*, as the name of a rocket. He understands why a judge's decision is likened to Solomon's or a city is called Sodom or a business man is labeled a Babbitt.

In college, knowledge of such literature is taken for granted, just as primitive societies took for granted that its young members knew the rituals of the people. The primitive rituals were well formalized. But, unfortunately, the list of books that make up the reservoir of literature for our culture is not so formalized. No two people include exactly the same titles when listing materials that all young people should know. However, the following list is fairly representative of what one should read before entering college:

1. *The Mother Goose Rhymes:* These were originally political satires, but by the eighteenth century they were sung regularly and recited to children in English nurseries. In America additional ones have been added, such as "Mary Had a Little Lamb."

2. *The Basic Fairy Stories:* The most familiar of these are the French fairy stories written by Charles

Perrault, a courtier in Louis XIV's court. These include *Cinderella, Little Red Riding Hood, Sleeping Beauty, Puss in Boots, Hop-O-My-Thumb, Bluebeard, Diamonds and Toads.* A few other classic fairy stories have become part of the tradition: *Jack and the Beanstalk, The Three Bears, Chicken Little, Peter Rabbit, Little Black Sambo, Epaminondas.* The very literary and beautiful stories of Hans Christian Andersen and the very folksy *Uncle Remus Stories,* by Joel Chandler Harris, complete this list of material.

3. *Aesop's Fables:* The animal fables, each with its rather heavy-handed moral, have become almost universally known in Western culture. *The Boy Who Cried Wolf* and *The Fox and the Grapes* are examples of Aesop's tales.

4. *The Greek Myths:* While it is difficult to keep all the family relationships among the Greek gods and goddesses in order, some familiarity with the ancient Greek stories of the Olympians is important for an appreciation of both classic and contemporary literature.

5. *The Iliad and the Odyssey:* The stories of the Trojan War and Odysseus (called Ulysses by the Romans) and of his long voyage home are the source of a continuing body of legend.

6. *Greek Tragedy:* Out of the hundreds of tragedies produced in Ancient Greece only twenty or so have survived. These plays are highly structured to produce the emotional impact called "catharsis," that few other dramatists have succeeded in evoking. At least one of the Greek tragedies should be read. The best known is probably *Oedipus Rex,* by Sophocles.

7. *The Bible:* Certainly the most familiar of the Bible stories should become a part of the child's cultural inheritance regardless of his religion. The stories of Moses, of David, of Isaac, of Ruth, of Esther, of Job, and the parables of the New Testament are all inextricably woven through Western literature and

philosophy. Furthermore the rhythm of biblical language has had a significant impact on the rhythm of our language as a whole.

8. Alice in Wonderland: It is strange that a book originally intended as a children's story should have found its main audience among adults. The land down the Rabbit's hole and the land behind the looking glass are familiar places for adults as well as children.

9. Robinson Crusoe: The story of Crusoe's adventure as a castaway on a desert island has remained the classic story of the individual who survives because he uses his wits. So real is Crusoe to most people that tourists today are shown his island off the coast of South America.

10. Little Women: Few males but most females cherish the delightful family life of the Marches, who experience happiness, privation, death, and love.

11. Pilgrim's Progress: Perhaps less read today than in earlier generations, *Pilgrim's Progress* still introduces students to such familiar concepts as Vanity Fair, the Slough of Despond, the Narrow Gate, the Straight Road, etc.

12. Don Quixote: While few people actually read the whole of *Don Quixote,* they come to know the story through abridged versions. So firmly is this erratic knight embedded in Western consciousness that his name has given the word *quixotic* to the English language.

13. Gulliver's Travels: Gulliver makes four voyages in all, each structured as a vitriolic attack on some defects in man's nature. But so charmingly are the tales told that they have become favorites of most children. The two most important to read are the "Voyage to the Land of the Lilliputians" and "The Voyage to the Land of the Brobdingnags."

14. Shakespeare: Shakespeare is so bound into our culture that it is hard to conceive of our literature or our lives without him. The easiest plays for students to read and comprehend are *A Midsummer Night's Dream, Romeo and Juliet,* and *The Merchant of Venice.* The four great tragedies—*Julius Caesar, Macbeth, King Lear* and *Hamlet*—are even more important in the cultural reservoir of our literature than are the comedies and histories.

15. *Uncle Tom's Cabin:* This powerful antislavery novel may have been the match that ignited the Civil War; it is still widely read and enjoyed by many. It tells a good story and captures the reader in spite of its obvious sentimentality.

16. *British Novels of the Nineteenth Century:* The British writers of this period produced a flood of fiction filled with vivid characters and exciting experiences. Excellent novels to read are *Pride and Prejudice, Jane Eyre, Wuthering Heights, Vanity Fair, The Mayor of Casterbridge, Great Expectations, David Copperfield,* and *The Mill on the Floss.*

17. *Mark Twain:* No one, of course, has ever caught so vividly the delights of a boy's life in a small midcontinent town of America as does Mark Twain in *Tom Sawyer.* It is no wonder that Tom and Huck Finn are as real to most adults as the schoolmates with whom they grew up. Mark Twain was haunted by the idea that basically people are interchangeable; only the trappings of their life make them different. This idea is most forcefully caught in his story of *The Prince and the Pauper* and has colored American thinking about people's real virtues ever since.

18. *Other American Novels of the Nineteenth Century:* The American writers of this period created novels peculiarly American. Required reading are such books as *The Scarlet Letter, Moby Dick, Huckleberry Finn, The Red Badge of Courage, Ethan Frome, The Rise of Silas Lapham.*

19. *Continental Fiction:* A few works of Continental fiction are also indispensable reading for the college-bound student. *Les Misérables,* the French story of

poverty and deprivation during the nineteenth century, and *Crime and Punishment*, the previously mentioned Russian novel that details the anguish of a student who has murdered a pawnbroker, are two examples.

20. *Twentieth-century Novels:* These were discussed in Chapter 8. If a student has read this central body of literature by the time he graduates from high school, he will have a good background for his college work. It is obvious, though, that to accomplish this amount of reading it is necessary for the youngster to begin early and not to leave it for a last-minute crash reading program.

The ordering of the material is fairly obvious. In the early elementary school years, the child should be exposed to Mother Goose, the fairy stories, and the animal fables. In late elementary school, he will enjoy the Greek myths, the Bible stories, *Gulliver's Travels*, *Don Quixote* (in an abridged form), *Tom Sawyer* and *The Prince and the Pauper*. Many people try to force *Alice in Wonderland* at this period, but unfortunately many children find it frightening. The book is probably most successful at the senior level in high school.

In junior high school, the college-bound student is ready for *Robinson Crusoe*, *Uncle Tom's Cabin*, the *Iliad* and the *Odyssey*, *A Midsummer Night's Dream*, *Romeo and Juliet*, and perhaps *Pilgrim's Progress*. It is best for most youngsters to wait until the last two years of high school to tackle the Greek tragedies, the great Shakespearean tragedies, and the nineteenth-century novels of America and England.

Through normal patterns of reading development, a high school student should, by his senior year, have discovered twentieth-century literature and sampled works by Sinclair Lewis, Ernest Hemingway, John Steinbeck, Thomas Wolfe, Joseph Conrad, William Golding, F. Scott Fitzgerald, Graham Greene, Franz Kafka, Albert Camus, and J. D. Salinger.

A number of the philosophic and humanistic issues

of all times are discussed in drama more vividly than
in any other art form. High school English courses require the reading of Sheridan's *She Stoops to Conquer,*
and Thornton Wilder's *Our Town,* as well as Greek
drama and some Shakespeare. But it would be a
splendid idea to encourage your adolescent to read
something by Molière, O'Neill, perhaps one or two of
Ibsen's plays, and some by Tennessee Williams, Arthur
Miller, and Jean-Paul Sartre.

Because the study of literature will be only a small
part of most students' college work, it is important that
adolescents read other kinds of material as well, particularly in areas not usually a part of the high school
curriculum. Readable books in psychology, philosophy,
history and criticism of the arts, anthropology, and
archaeology will introduce the student to the subjects
he will study in college courses.

There are, of course, many published lists of books
for college preparation. Many colleges and universities
have prepared such lists for their entering freshmen.
These can usually be obtained by writing to the regis-
trars of colleges which your child is considering. The
list of classics given at the end of Chapter 9 is typical
of the titles that appear as recommended reading. You
can use it with the assurance that it will prove a good
guide. The National Council of Teachers of English,
the largest group of subject-matter teachers in the
world, publishes a book entitled *The College and
Adult Reading List.* The list covers approximately 760
titles, each with a fairly extensive annotation including
a brief critical opinion. The subtitle indicates the
limits of the list's coverage: *Books in Literature and
the Fine Arts.* A student might make use of this broad
list by attempting to read at least one book in each of
the forty major subdivisions. The American Library
Association also has a short pamphlet of books for college-bound students. These two lists together represent the pooled opinions of two national organizations

about titles worth considering by the college-bound student.

But regardless of any specific books that a student has read, he is not really ready for college unless he has developed the following attitudes and habits:

1. *He thoroughly enjoys reading.* He will devote a part of almost every day to reading for his own satisfaction. When he is enmeshed in a book, he will sometimes stay up half the night to finish it. And when he finishes a book, he occasionally shares his reactions by talking about it. Then he goes on a prowl to find another book to begin. For this young person books are a normal part of daily living. Even though your child may not have read the books listed earlier in this chapter, if he reads with avidness and enthusiasm, he may be better prepared for college than the youngster who has forced himself to read a prescribed list of books because he feels it is necessary for college entrance. It is for this reason that throughout the chapters of this volume so much stress has been placed on helping the adolescent find books of intrinsic interest to him rather than pressuring him into reading the works we feel "worthwhile."

2. *He reads for two different purposes.* In other words, he reads for pleasure at certain times and for information at other times. The student who will succeed in college is the one who has discovered that books offer escape, refreshment, and delight, but that they may also supply information. The person who reads for only one purpose is actually a "reading cripple." It is valuable for the young person to develop the habit of turning to books to find an answer to a puzzling question or to explore a new idea. Occasionally he may become so fascinated with a nonfiction book about a subject new to him that he will read it, spellbound whether it is information about the workings of computers, the history of the ancient Mayas, or ways to look at a painting.

3. The books he selects are relatively mature. The
level of maturity which your child has reached can be
fairly accurately judged by a knowledge of the reading
patterns discussed in this book. The student who is
ready for college should be reading serious modern
literature fairly regularly and should occasionally seek
out and read some of the classics. His choices will not,
of course, be consistent. It would be most unusual if
he did not occasionally drop back and read a shoot-
'em-up spy story or a romantic love story just for the
fun of it. But unless he can find personal satisfaction in
the two types of reading at the top of the reading scale,
he will have some difficulties with the reading assignments that he will face in college. He should, in addition, be able to read involved expository writing
without having his mind wander off to other things.
You might suggest he sometimes try an article from
magazines such as *Harper's, The Atlantic Monthly,* or
The Saturday Review. And he should be encouraged
to pick up a book about music or anthropology or
politics and finish it, because unless he can handle this
type of material he may find the style of college texts
almost beyond his comprehension.

Reading for college preparation, then, is not something that can wait for the last minute. It is a program
that should encompass the entire reading life of the
child. While it is desirable that he read as much as he
can of the common cultural reservoir of literature, it
is even more important that he find reading enjoyable
and that he develop good attitudes and habits towards
this skill. Hence a good preparation for college does
not mean that a youngster jumps the gun by trying to
read college material ahead of time. Instead it means
giving him the assurance that he can handle mature
materials in a variety of styles with ease and comprehension.

Bibliography

Many schools and colleges make available to their students a selected list of books recommended or required for the college bound. The books included here represent those titles that most frequently appear on many of these lists. Several of these lists were, in fact, substantial surveys made by such groups as The Wisconsin Council of Teachers of English, the Adult Services Division of the New York Library Association, the New England Association of Teachers of English, the Lucas County Library in Maumee, Ohio, and the Pennsylvania College presidents and faculties.

In using such a list, the parent needs to keep in mind that a boy or girl has only a limited amount of time for reading after he has completed the assignments normally given him for his four or five classes. He can perhaps manage to read an "additional" book about once a month. This means that he can read, at most, ten to fifteen books a year. All lists include many more titles than any one student can possibly read. Therefore, let your youngster be highly selective in sampling from the list; it is not necessary to read through it systematically.

Furthermore it is important that the parent and adult distinguish between reading as "preparation" for college and reading that will normally be done in college. Too often the assumption is that a student should read everything he will be assigned in college before he arrives. Works like the *Divine Comedy*, the *Canterbury Tales*, and Plato's *Republic*, for example, are usually read *in* college. There is no reason why the entering student should have read them already. In fact he may have the excitement taken from college work if he has done so.

FICTION AND POETRY

Agee, James: *A Death in the Family.*
Anderson, Sherwood: *Winesburg, Ohio.*
Austen, Jane: *Pride and Prejudice.*
Baldwin, James: *Go Tell It on the Mountain.*

Balzac, Honoré de: *Père Goriot.*
Bronte, Charlotte: *Jane Eyre.*
Bronte, Emily: *Wuthering Heights.*
Buck, Pearl: *The Good Earth.*
Bunyan, John: *Pilgrim's Progress.*
Camus, Albert: *The Stranger.*
Carroll, Lewis: *Alice in Wonderland.*
Cather, Willa: *Death Comes for the Archbishop; My Ántonia.*
Cervantes, Miguel de: *Don Quixote.*
Clemens, Samuel: *See* Twain, Mark.
Conrad, Joseph: *Heart of Darkness.*
————: *Lord Jim.*
Cooper, James F.: *Last of the Mohicans.*
Crane, Stephen: *The Red Badge of Courage.*
Defoe, Daniel: *Robinson Crusoe.*
Dickens, Charles: *David Copperfield.*
————: *Great Expectations.*
————: *Oliver Twist.*
————: *A Tale of Two Cities.*
Dostoevski, Fyodor: *Crime and Punishment.*
————: *The Brothers Karamazov.*
Dreiser, Theodore: *An American Tragedy.*
Dumas, Alexandre: *The Count of Monte Cristo.*
————: *The Three Musketeers.*
Eliot, George: *Mill on the Floss.*
Faulkner, William: *Intruder in the Dust.*
————: *The Sound and The Fury.*
Fielding, Henry: *Tom Jones.*
Fitzgerald, F. Scott: *The Great Gatsby.*
Flaubert, Gustav: *Madame Bovary.*
Forster, E. M.: *A Passage to India.*
Frost, Robert: *Poems.*
Hardy, Thomas: *The Mayor of Casterbridge.*
————: *Tess of the D'Urbervilles.*
Hawthorne, Nathaniel: *The Scarlet Letter.*
Hemingway, Ernest: *A Farewell to Arms.*
————: *For Whom the Bell Tolls.*
————: *The Old Man and the Sea.*
————: *The Sun Also Rises.*
Homer: *Iliad.*
————: *Odyssey.*
Hudson, W. H.: *Green Mansions.*
Hugo, Victor: *The Hunchback of Notre Dame.*
————: *Les Misérables.*

Huxley, Aldous: *Brave New World.*
James, Henry: *The Turn of the Screw.*
Koestler, Arthur: *Darkness at Noon.*
Lawrence, D. H.: *Sons and Lovers.*
Lederer, W. J., and Eugene Burdick: *The Ugly American.*
Lee, Harper: *To Kill a Mockingbird.*
Lewis, Sinclair: *Arrowsmith.*
————: *Babbitt.*
————: *Main Street.*
London, Jack: *The Call of the Wild.*
Malory, Thomas: *Le Morte d'Arthur.*
Maugham, Somerset: *Of Human Bondage.*
Melville, Herman: *Moby Dick.*
Nordhoff, Charles, and James Hall: *Mutiny on the Bounty.*
Orwell, George: *Animal Farm.*
————: *1984.*
Paton, Alan: *Cry, the Beloved Country.*
Rawlings, Marjorie Kinnan: *The Yearling.*
Remarque, Erich Maria: *All Quiet on the Western Front.*
Roberts, Kenneth: *Northwest Passage.*
Rolvaag, O. E.: *Giants in the Earth.*
Saint-Exupéry, Antoine de: *Wind, Sand and Stars.*
Salinger, J. D.: *The Catcher in the Rye.*
Scott, Sir Walter: *Ivanhoe.*
Sienkiewicz, Henryk: *Quo Vadis.*
Steinbeck, John: *The Grapes of Wrath.*
————: *Of Mice and Men.*
Stevenson, Robert Louis: *Kidnapped.*
————: *Treasure Island.*
Stowe, Harriet Beecher: *Uncle Tom's Cabin.*
Thackeray, William Makepeace: *Vanity Fair.*
Twain, Mark: *The Adventures of Huckleberry Finn.*
————: *The Adventures of Tom Sawyer.*
————: *A Connecticut Yankee in King Arthur's Court.*
————: *Life on the Mississippi.*
Turgenev, Ivan: *Fathers and Sons.*
Voltaire: *Candide.*
Warren, Robert Penn: *All the King's Men.*
Wharton, Edith: *Ethan Frome.*
Wolfe, Thomas: *Look Homeward, Angel.*
————: *You Can't Go Home Again.*
Wouk, Herman: *The Caine Mutiny.*

DRAMA

Anderson, Maxwell: *Mary of Scotland*.
Chekhov, Anton: *The Cherry Orchard*.
————: *Three Sisters*.
Connelly, Mark: *Green Pastures*.
Eliot, T. S.: *The Cocktail Party*.
————: *Murder in the Cathedral*.
Euripides: *Medea*.
Fry, Christopher: *The Lady's Not for Burning*.
Hellman, Lillian: *The Little Foxes*.
Ibsen Henrik: *The Doll's House*.
————: *Hedda Gabler*.
MacLeish, Archibald: *J.B.*
Marlowe, Christopher: *Doctor Faustus*.
Miller, Arthur: *Death of a Salesman*.
O'Neill, Eugene: *Ah, Wilderness!*
————: *The Emperor Jones*.
————: *Mourning Becomes Electra*.
Rostand, Edmond: *Cyrano de Bergerac*.
Shakespeare, William: *Antony and Cleopatra*.
————: *Hamlet*.
————: *King Henry IV*.
————: *King Henry V*.
————: *King Lear*.
————: *Macbeth*.
————: *The Merchant of Venice*.
————: *A Midsummer Night's Dream*.
————: *Othello*.
————: *Richard II*.
————: *Romeo and Juliet*.
————: *The Tempest*.
————: *Twelfth Night*.
Shaw, George Bernard: *Androcles and the Lion*.
————: *Arms and the Man*.
————: *Caesar and Cleopatra*.
————: *Candida*.
————: *The Devil's Disciple*.
————: *Man and Superman*.
————: *Pygmalion*.
————: *St. Joan*.

Sophocles: *Antigone.*
———: *Oedipus Rex.*
Sheridan, Richard Brinsley: *The Rivals.*
Sherwood, Robert E.: *Abe Lincoln in Illinois.*
Synge, John: *Playboy of the Western World.*
Wilde, Oscar: *The Importance of Being Earnest.*
Wilder, Thornton: *Our Town.*
Williams, Tennessee: *The Glass Menagerie.*
———: *A Streetcar Named Desire.*

NONFICTION

Adams, Henry: *Mont St. Michel and Chartres.*
Baldwin, James: *Nobody Knows My Name.*
———: *Notes of a Native Son.*
Barzun, Jacques: *The House of Intellect.*
Benedict, Ruth: *Patterns of Culture.*
Boswell, James: *Life of Johnson.*
Bowen, Catherine Drinker: *Yankee from Olympus.*
Bulfinch, Thomas: *The Age of Fable.*
Carson, Rachel: *The Sea Around Us.*
Conant, James: *Modern Science and Modern Man.*
Curie, Eve: *Madame Curie.*
De Tocqueville, Alexis: *Democracy in America.*
Durant, Will: *The Story of Civilization; The Story of Philos-
     ophy.*
Fermi, Laura: *Atoms in the Family.*
Franklin, Benjamin: *Autobiography.*
Frazier, James George: *The Golden Bough.*
Galbraith, J. K.: *The Affluent Society.*
Gamow, George: *One, Two, Three . . . Infinity.*
Hamilton, Edith: *The Greek Way.*
Heilbroner, Robert: *Worldly Philosophers.*
Hersey, John: *Hiroshima.*
Hofstadter, Richard: *The American Political Tradition.*
Kluckhohn, Clyde: *Mirror for Man.*
Newman, James R., ed.: *What Is Science?*
Parkman, Francis: *The Oregon Trail.*
Plato: *Dialogues.*
———: *Republic.*
Plutarch: *Lives.*
Riesman, David: *The Lonely Crowd.*

Rossiter, Clinton: *The American Presidency.*
Sandburg, Carl: *Abraham Lincoln.*
Scheinfeld, Amram: *You and Heredity.*
Schweitzer, Albert: *Out of My Life and Thought.*
Shirer, William: *Rise and Fall of the Third Reich.*
Snow, C. P.: *The Two Cultures and the Scientific Revolution.*
Strunk, William: *Elements of Style.*
Thoreau, Henry David: *Walden.*
Virgil: *The Aeneid.*
White, Theodore: *The Making of the President 1960.*
Whitehead, Alfred North: *Science and the Modern World.*
————: *Aims of Education and Other Essays.*
Whyte, William H.: *The Organization Man.*

Chapter 14
A *Guide* to *Reference Books*

Curiosity is, in great and generous minds, the first passion and the last.

Samuel Johnson, *The Rambler*

One of the greatest qualities that we can foster in our children is a questing mind. The person who is constantly asking questions and who learns where and how to find answers is the one who is growing. He grows as a human personality, he grows in his human relationships, and he grows in his vocational competence. On the other hand, an individual may drift with the processes of living. He may simply accept the daily round of activities as they come, involving himself only with what is immediately demanding. Unfortunately, too many people in our twentieth-century civilization are willing to let life and knowledge surge around them, but never permit any meaningful contact.

Every child is born with a desire to explore the world around him. Shortly after he learns to talk, he starts to ask questions. Every parent is bombarded with "why?" "how?" and "what?" questions by his preschool child. Later as the child progresses through school, his questions become more specific: "Where did Columbus actually land?" "What does *serendipity* mean?" "Where was the Golden Crescent?" "Who assassinated McKinley?"

Whether the child continues to ask questions depends to a considerable extent on how adults in his immediate world react to his questioning. If they laugh at him, if they shrug the question off with an "I haven't an idea" attitude, if they ignore him completely, he will learn rather quickly that questions are not socially acceptable in his world. He will sense through a parent's indifference that it is better not to question. But the parent who says, "Well, let's look up the answer," who goes with the child to an encyclopedia, a dictionary, an atlas, and helps the child find the answer, is bound to foster the child's natural curiosity. This youngster will feel that books are important, that questions count.

Most questions arise unexpectedly out of the give and take of everyday living, out of conversations, articles in the daily newspaper, references on TV, and the like. This momentary flash of curiosity is seldom strong enough to be kept alive until the adolescent has a chance to go to a library. Therefore it is important for a home to have good reference materials. Some families even keep dictionaries and encyclopedias near the dining room table so that whenever a dinner discussion bogs down in ignorance over a particular point or fact there is a reliable source to turn to for the answer.

Reference books—good reference books—are expensive. However, the family which can afford to drive an automobile probably can afford to buy the reference books that will nurture the child's curiosity. Good sets of reference material are not much more expensive than poor ones. Having good reference books is important, for the child who turns expectantly to look up material, only to find no answer to his question, will probably develop a distrust of books rather than excitement about them.

Because reference books are relatively expensive, it is important that you not be stampeded into making a selection. A door-to-door salesman can be highly persuasive in displaying his wares. Before making any such purchase, you should collect facts about the possible alternatives. Almost any good school library or public library will have several different sets of encyclopedias so that you can lay out the competing sets on a table and compare them. The librarian will also have a good deal of sound advice to offer and may direct you to *The Subscription Books Bulletin,* published by the American Library Association, which evaluates these materials.

The most fundamental reference that the adolescent should have at hand is a good dictionary. There are roughly three levels of dictionaries among which to choose. There is the unabridged dictionary of the language: this dictionary attempts to record and classify every word that is used by native speakers of the English language. Funk and Wagnalls' *New Standard Dictionary of the English Language* (1959) and G. & C. Merriam's *Webster's Third New International Dictionary of the English Language, Unabridged* (1961) are both excellent examples of such works. Each is expensive, costing between forty and fifty dollars. The new *Random House Dictionary of the English Language* is priced lower, around twenty-five dollars. For a family with some scholarly inclinations, the unabridged dictionary is a worthwhile purchase; but it has the disadvantage of being too large to be portable. This means it must stand on a desk or at some fixed place in the home.

So for general, everyday use, the second level of dictionary, the desk dictionary, is more useful. A number of these are designated as "college" dictionaries, indicating that they are basic tools for the person who is pursuing the normal kinds of higher education. Such a dictionary usually defines between 120,000 to 150,000 words, approximately a fourth of the total number in the language. However, very few people ever find themselves hunting for a word that is not included in this basic selection. Recommended college dictionaries are Funk and Wagnalls' *Standard College Dictionary,* G. & C. Merriam's *Webster's New Collegiate Dictionary,* World's *Webster's New World Dictionary of the American Language* (College Edition), Random House's *American College Dictionary.* Each of these has certain distinct features, but each is highly recommended and is a worthwhile purchase. Differences among these works are in the format—the way the words are labeled as colloquial, slang, or formal; whether biographical and geographical material is in a separate section or included in the main body; the emphasis on recent scientific terminology; and the system for marking the pronunciation of the words. Such matters are largely dependent on one's personal tastes, and most average users will not realize that the differences exist. Once a dictionary is used for a few weeks' time, its peculiarities become familiar and acceptable.

The third level of dictionary is designed for the younger person, in elementary and secondary school. This type of dictionary has a still more limited number of words, usually including between 35,000 and 70,000 words. This covers about one-tenth of the words in the English language. The limitation seems severe, but research has disclosed that about 2,000 words make up 95 per cent of the words that the average person uses in his writing. Besides having fewer words, the school dictionaries give less information about each word and fewer meanings for individual items; and at times the word derivation information is eliminated.

School dictionaries are much easier for the young teen-ager to use than the big volumes, and they may be attractively illustrated. Perhaps the most widely used of these dictionaries in the schools themselves are those published by Scott, Foresman & Company, under the editorship of Thorndike and Barnhart. Most useful for the adolescent are the *Thorndike-Barnhart Advanced Junior Dictionary* and the *Thorndike-Barnhart High School Dictionary.* Since these dictionaries have been through a number of editions, their contents have been refined and winnowed for maximum serviceability. Less forbidding in appearance, these dictionaries with their larger print, less fragile paper, and attractive illustrations encourage the junior high school student in the "dictionary habit." Unfortunately the adult dictionary can sometimes drive the young person away from using it by the difficulty encountered in finding the word and the overwhelming amount of information which is more than he can readily absorb.

When buying a dictionary, there are a few criteria to keep in mind. First of all, it is important that you buy an American dictionary rather than a British one. All those mentioned in this chapter are American. There are some differences in the language of the two countries. One of the major differences lies in the spellings of certain words. The dictionary selected should be up-to-date. In science and technology new terminology is constantly being added to the language for the new discoveries, processes, and products. These words are often exactly the terms that the student needs to look up. Therefore maximum serviceability can be guaranteed only by the book with a copyright date no more than five years old. Third, you will be safest if you buy a dictionary published by a reputable company such as those mentioned. The word *Webster* is no guarantee of a good dictionary. Noah Webster was a schoolmaster and scholar living during the first half of the nineteenth century. He not only wrote spellers and readers, but he undertook a dictionary of the English language which passed through various editions during his life and became the accepted work of this type. It is interesting to note that his dictionary contained only 70,000 entries, about the number found in the average dictionary geared for the adolescent. After Webster's death, revisions were done by the G. & C. Merriam Co., but the name *Webster* became synonymous with the word *dictionary*. Since there is no copyright on using the name, a number of companies use the name Webster in their titles. This is no guarantee of their reliability. Some are reputable reference books, others are not.

Fortunately, there are several excellent dictionaries in inexpensive paperback editions. Most good students will want a copy of either *Webster's New World Dictionary*, the *New Merriam-Webster Pocket Dictionary*, or the *Thorndike-Barnhart Dictionary*.

The encyclopedia is a second reference tool. Because it represents a major expenditure, it should be considered with great care. While not as clearly differentiated into levels as the dictionaries, there are still roughly three levels of encyclopedia: the adult and scholarly encyclopedia; the family encyclopedia; the junior encyclopedia. The following information may help you decide which one will best serve your family's purposes and whether you should consider buying encyclopedias on two different levels.

The two most scholarly encyclopedias are the *Britannica* and the *Americana*. The following chart highlights some of the differences between the two.

Name of encyclopedia	Number of articles	Type of article	Number of words	Number of words to one illustration
BRITANNICA	35,000	Broad	36 million	2,045
AMERICANA	69,000	Specific	28½ million	1,575

As you can see, the *Britannica* has several million more words but only half as many articles. It organizes its material into fairly broad topics whereas the *Americana* breaks knowledge into smaller segments. Of the two, the *Americana* is more profusely illustrated. *Britannica* is the older of the two encyclopedias and traditionally has been considered the more scholarly, but also the more leisurely in style. It tends to emphasize the humanities and British subjects while the *Americana* tends to stress science, technology, and American subjects. For example, *Britannica* gives more space to the Canadian provinces than to the individual states of our country. However, *Britannica* is now under American ownership and an effort is being made to popularize its style and format, to include more illustrations, and to give greater coverage to the United States.

The second level of encyclopedia is the family set. This group of references attempts to meet the needs of the average adult who wants ready information in clear journalistic style on many subjects about which questions arise daily. A mother may want to know the symptoms of a particular childhood disease or the man of the house may want information on the founding of modern Israel. The scholarly encyclopedias may provide the same information but in more detail than a casual reader wants. Of the family encyclopedias, *Collier's Encyclopedia* is perhaps the foremost contender. It contains 22 million words, which is 7 million less than the *Americana* and 14 million less than the *Britannica*. Its articles are broadly conceived, its style of writing less difficult to understand than that of the *Britannica* or the *Americana*, and it is more profusely illustrated. It has been so well received that both the *Britannica* and the *Americana* have tended in their recent revisions to move in the direction set by *Collier's*.

The third level of encyclopedia is the young people's or student's encyclopedia. There are three that are recommended: the *World Book, Britannica Junior* and *Compton's*. A table similar to that given for the scholarly encyclopedias may help highlight the salient differences among these three sets.

Name of encyclopedia	Number of articles	Type of article	Number of words	Number of words to one illustration
WORLD BOOK	30,000	Specific	8.5 million	350
COMPTON'S	4,000	Broad	7.7 million	410
BRITANNICA	4,000	Broad	5 million	510

World Book differs from the other two by breaking its topics into more specific categories. These are arranged in alphabetical order. Thus the makers of *World Book* claim that a young reader does not have to use a special index to find the material he is seeking. He simply looks at the code letters on the back of each volume to find the subject he wants. The other two

encyclopedias have far fewer articles, and hence each
article must cover a broader subject. In *World Book,*
for example, there is an article on the Navaho Indians
in the *N* volume. In *Compton's* the Navahos are
treated in a much longer article on Indians in the *I*
volume.

You will notice from the figures given that *Britannica Junior* is more limited than either *Compton's* or
World Book in the number of words. The publishers
of *Britannica* designed the jr. volume as an upper
elementary school encyclopedia. They felt adolescents
should be able to move directly to the use of the senior
Britannica. Recently, however, *Britannica* has purchased *Compton's* and is using it as a bridge between
Britannica Junior and the adult set.

World Book has often been sold as a family encyclopedia. Although far more limited in number of words
than *Compton's* and therefore in its possible coverage,
it has been successful for many families' general needs.

The only single-volume encyclopedia that is worth
buying is *The Columbia Encyclopedia, Third Edition.*
While it is still not cheap, it is far less expensive than
the multivolumed sets. Obviously, its coverage is far
more limited. But it is nevertheless authoritative in the
material included.

Following is a list of criteria to consider when purchasing an encyclopedia:

1. *Check to see that the set has a policy of continu-
ous revision.* All of the encyclopedias mentioned in
this chapter do. This means that year by year, articles
are brought up to date and new material added in
supplementary books rather than the company's continuing to issue the same book for, say, a ten-year
period and then doing a major revision of the set. By
purchasing a set that is continuously revised, you do
not have to worry that a new revision will suddenly
make yours outmoded.

2. *Beware of high-pressure salesmen that try to force
you to make up your mind instantly.* A really reputable

salesman will tell the advantages of his set and allow you time to do some checking on your own.

3. *Check with your school or public librarian to see which sets are most often used in the library.* These librarians also have sound information about encyclopedias in general.

4. *Check to see that the encyclopedia contains a list of authors and contributors of articles and their qualifications.* A good encyclopedia is written by scholars and authorities in each field.

5. *Check the binding and paper.* These books must withstand constant thumbing for a long period of time. Therefore these volumes need maximum durability.

6. *Find out who prepared the maps.* These should be done by some reputable atlas company such as Hammond or Rand McNally.

7. *Sample the encyclopedia to see how you like it.* Think of a question that you would like to know about. It might be, "How do fireflies produce their light?" Then see the process you must follow to find the information. Such an experiment demonstrates the ease, tone, and accessibility of material.

There are still other reference materials that may be found useful in the home. An earlier form of reference book that has its modern equivalent is the almanac. This is a yearly publication containing useful information about the immediate present. In the early days it was based on astrological predictions and gave prognostications about the weather—good days and bad days, growing conditions, dates for planting and reaping, and the like. The modern almanac is a kind of statistical yearbook containing somewhat conglomerate information. There are lists of award winners, names of state and foreign officials, the names and locations of schools, population figures, average temperatures, rainfall, and other facts and statistics. The two most reputable almanacs are the *Information Please Almanac* and *The World Almanac*. Both are available in paperbound editions for the immediate year, and cost about $2. Almanac readers are a special breed. Quite a number of intellectually curious people find a particular joy in the diverse information included in the almanac and browse in it for pleasure. Most persons turn to the almanac for the kind of immediate statistical information that answers a specific question.

An atlas is another reference source important for an adolescent. To be sure, most of its information can also be found in the encyclopedia, the almanac, and the dictionary if all three are used together, but the atlas pulls the geographic information together into one source. The principal mapmakers are C. S. Hammond & Co. and Rand McNally & Co. Both publish their own atlases. They also make maps used in many other publications including the major encyclopedias. *Encyclopedia Britannica* and the *World Book* both publish their own separate atlases. An atlas costs in the neighborhood of $10 to $15.

What makes an atlas good or mediocre? A good atlas should contain both political maps of the world showing boundaries of the countries, positions of the cities, and the like, and physical maps detailing the rivers, mountain ranges, relative altitudes, and other geographic features. Many maps contain both kinds of information, but a good atlas will have separate maps to present each kind. American atlases generally have individual maps for each of the states, but will not include individual maps for the states or provinces of the other countries of the world. Some atlases contain historical maps showing how the political boundaries of the world have shifted through the years. Many have a good deal of basic information about the population of the major cities and countries.

In purchasing an atlas be sure to check the completeness and usability of the index. Ease of use is most important for the beginner. Also note the date of publication, since an atlas even five years old is out of date in today's rapidly changing world. Naturally it is important to look at some of the maps to see whether a scale of miles is given, whether the printing is clear and easily read, and whether the physical features stand out.

Another possible family reference tool is the book of quotations. An individual finds he needs a specific quotation (usually a literary one) for a certain speech, for some writing he is doing, or to celebrate one of the special days of the year. The standard source is a reference book of quotations. For over a hundred years, people have used *Bartlett's Familiar Quotations* for just this purpose. It is periodically revised and now contains 1,069 pages of quotes. It sells for $10. Quotations are arranged by author in chronological order. The index at the back of the book is a concordance index: quotations are identified both by the first word and by the key thought. Thus if you want a quotation about *mother* or *fire* or *dogs* you can quickly locate those available in the book by looking under these subjects.

A second reputable book of quotations is Stevenson's *Home Book of Quotations*. It contains 73,000 quotes arranged topically under such headings as *love, religion, government,* etc. There is both an author and a concordance index at the back of the book.

Some families find the need for two other kinds of reference tools: one of these is a dictionary of usage. Frequently the problem arises of whether one should use *can* or *may* or say *likely, liable,* or *apt,* or whether one should answer *It's me.* Such problems are problems of usage. Newer dictionaries tend to describe the language, not to rule on it. A dictionary of usage will provide ready information about the status of such items as the above in the present language. Two of the most reputable ones are Margaret Bryant's *Current American Usage,* published by Funk & Wagnalls and H. W. Fowler's classic, *A Dictionary of Modern English Usage,* published by the Oxford University Press. Many people will be surprised to find that these authors rule as acceptable some expressions that schoolteachers still fuss about. It is helpful for a student to have the weight of a linguistic authority behind him in his decisions about usage.

Many people have found a dictionary of synonyms useful when they are looking for alternative words in writing or planning a speech. The classic book in this field is Roget's *Thesaurus for English Words and Phrases.* Over a hundred and fifty years ago Dr. Peter Mark Roget collected synonyms for his own use, and his son and grandson carried on the work with extended editions throughout the nineteenth century. Now new editions are regularly issued. Roget worked out an elaborate system for classification of human knowledge. An alphabetical listing of words in the back directs the user to the various categories in which the word may be found. There are many editions in hardcover and softcover.

In addition to the standard types of reference material discussed here, there are specialized reference tools in almost every subject matter field: in music, science, the social sciences, literature, arts, etc. If you have a son or daughter with a particular interest in a specialized field, you might check with a local librarian to find what kinds of information guides are available to give the ready information that might satisfy such interests.

When the basic necessities of life have been purchased, standard reference tools should probably come next in the family budget. They provide the introduction to the whole world of human strivings, discoveries, and accumulated knowledge. The adolescent needs to develop the habit of pursuing the answers to the questions that arise in his mind instead of constantly pushing them aside because it is too difficult to find the answer. The reference habit is built in the home through the constant use of a few basic tools. Once established, it probably does more to further the academic success of the adolescent than anything else.